T0365231

Cambridge Elements

Elements in Publishing and Book Culture
edited by
Samantha J. Rayner
University College London
Leah Tether
University of Bristol

THE FORM AND THEORY OF LITERARY DOODLING

Jeremiah R. Mercurio
Columbia University, New York

Daniel Gabelman
King's Ely

Shaftesbury Road, Cambridge CB2 8EA, United Kingdom

One Liberty Plaza, 20th Floor, New York, NY 10006, USA

477 Williamstown Road, Port Melbourne, VIC 3207, Australia

314–321, 3rd Floor, Plot 3, Splendor Forum, Jasola District Centre,
New Delhi – 110025, India

103 Penang Road, #05–06/07, Visioncrest Commercial, Singapore 238467

Cambridge University Press is part of Cambridge University Press & Assessment,
a department of the University of Cambridge.

We share the University's mission to contribute to society through the pursuit
of education, learning and research at the highest international levels of excellence.

www.cambridge.org
Information on this title: www.cambridge.org/9781009492430

DOI: 10.1017/9781009492416

When citing this work, please include a reference to the DOI 10.1017/9781009492416

First published 2025

A catalogue record for this publication is available from the British Library

ISBN 978-1-009-49243-0 Paperback
ISSN 2514-8524 (online)
ISSN 2514-8516 (print)

The Form and Theory of Literary Doodling

Elements in Publishing and Book Culture

DOI: 10.1017/9781009492416
First published online: February 2025

Jeremiah R. Mercurio
Columbia University, New York

Daniel Gabelman
King's Ely

Author for correspondence: Jeremiah R. Mercurio, jrm2282@columbia.edu

Abstract: This Element investigates the phenomenon of literary doodling – the making of playful verbal and visual creations by professional authors while engaged in another activity. The first part, Demarcation, focuses on defining the form and structure of doodles, comparing and contrasting them with adjacent genres such as sketches, caricatures, and illustrations. The second part, Exploration, explores the modality of doodling, examining doodles through the lenses of spectrality, liminality, and play. Drawing on a wide range of theories and backed up with numerous close readings, the Element argues that doodles, despite their apparent triviality, provide valuable insights into the creative processes, authorial habits, and finished works of literary doodlers. Ultimately, this study aims to legitimise doodles as worthy of serious critical attention, demonstrating how they trouble the meaning of texts, introduce semantic flexibility into literary works and their reception, and rejuvenate the joy of readerly discovery.

Keywords: doodles, literary doodling, marginalia, illustration, long nineteenth century

ISBNs: 9781009492430 (PB), 9781009492416 (OC)
ISSNs: 2514-8524 (online), 2514-8516 (print)

Contents

Introduction

Doodling might at first appear to be a strange subject for a scholarly treatise. After all, what could be more trivial, inconsequential, and inscrutable than those bizarre scribbles and sketches that adorn many schoolbooks, notepads, and journals – often signalling their creators' inattention and boredom? Understood in these terms, doodles seem to be fundamentally antithetical to analysis. Rather than intelligible symbols, they suggest more often than not a subconscious resistance to coherent discourse, a protest against the constraints of logic or discipline.

Yet doodles retain the ability to fascinate. We continue to interrogate them for hidden meanings and recognise their talismanic power to spur creation. Numerous popular books seek to harness this potency. Sunni Brown's *The Doodle Revolution: Unlock the Power to Think Differently* (2014) is a good example of this genre. An expansion of her popular TED talk on doodling as a method by which to develop visual literacy and proficiency, Brown's book sees doodles as aids to the construction of meaning – as 'spontaneous marks made to support thinking' (12). With this definition in hand, she cites examples of doodlers like Einstein, Tesla, and Steve Jobs – whose doodling (loosely defined) has 'given society huge, game-changing innovations' – to encourage everyone to 'see the doodle in a positive and functional way and then to capitalize on its magnificent utility' (12). Even skilled artists have alluded to the importance of doodling for the creation of visual art, emphasising the ways in which it 'engages the artist's imagination' (Doherty 2005, 28).

These popular explorations of doodling understand it as a playful and productive impulse. By letting go of inhibitions and embracing visual experimentation, one can discover new ideas and engage with the thoughts of others in ways unavailable through conscious attention and contemplation. While admitting that doodles can be useful tools for ideating, one can still ask what value they have for scholars. Even if the act of doodling can lead its practitioners to an insight or revelation of some sort, the doodles themselves are often unintelligible or highly ambiguous, making them resistant to scholarly interpretation. Like inkblots in a Rorschach test, doodles can also reveal more about the viewers than their creators.

What this Element calls *literary doodling* – the playful verbal and visual creations made by professional authors while engaged in another activity – differs from the more general practice of doodling in that it primarily accompanies the traditional labour of literary production: writing, reading, and note taking.[1] One finds doodles in the manuscripts, notebooks, and personal libraries of a surprising number of professional writers. At least at first glance, these doodles are often as ambiguous as their lay counterparts. Perhaps that is one reason relatively little critical attention has been paid to them, even when their creators are major literary figures such as Percy Bysshe Shelley, the Brontës, Mark Twain, Joseph Conrad, Marcel Proust, and James Joyce. Although authors such as these were prolific doodlers, their doodling often appears to be indecipherable or unrelated to (albeit collocated with) their traditional literary work. Ultimately, one might appreciate authors' doodles as mute traces of their mental activity while forsaking any hope of making sense of them.

Beyond their general obscurity, doodles figure infrequently in literary analysis because of their putative triviality. Doodles are seemingly unserious creations, and the act of doodling often suggests a goofing off, a delinquency of some sort that simultaneously departs from a more sober activity and undermines it. Think of the distracted doodling of someone in a business meeting. Critical discussions of doodling in relationship to literature, such as they exist, often refer pejoratively to verbal rather than visual forms of trifling. Some critics even use the term to draw distinctions between types of writing within authors' notebooks: between the serious writing found therein and the frivolous scribblings that are unworthy of scholarly attention. Paul J. Ferlazzo (2007) makes just such a distinction in summarising the value of Robert Frost's notebooks: 'Although some passages may appear as literary doodling, other items show the poet thinking and rethinking important ideas and beliefs.'

[1] 'Literary doodling' as a term is rare; however, it typically refers – by analogy to doodlistic sketches – to playful, frivolous, or experimental forms of writing and not to the more specific type of literary activity (verbal or visual) that we seek to define in this Element.

Ferlazzo implicitly defines doodling as unimportant and antithetical to 'thinking and rethinking' (i.e., as the absence of intelligible thought), a distinction that is itself yet another barrier to understanding doodles and their meanings. By placing inscrutability at the centre of their definitions, critics such as Ferlazzo effectively categorise doodles but also pre-empt further analysis. Doodling becomes the thing about which one 'cannot speak' – to borrow a phrase from Ludwig Wittgenstein's ((1921) 2023) famous ending to the *Tractatus Logico-Philosophicus* (68). Doodles either exist beyond language or represent a sort of nonsense language; thus, we are encouraged to observe them mutely and dumbly.

While acknowledging the limits inherent to analysing doodles, this Element nonetheless challenges the notion that little or nothing can be said about them and seeks instead to provide a critical foundation for the study of doodling. Despite their semantic complications, doodles are a distinct form of verbo-pictorial expression that possesses a grammar, an historical reality, and what in phenomenology might be called an horizon – that is, a context through which they can achieve meaningful representation. Those horizons – to channel Hans-Georg Gadamer – and those of their creators can be fused with the horizons of their interpreters to glean, create, and reshape the meaning of doodles.[2] That is to say, this study sets itself a goal of developing an interpretative framework for doodles that is flexible, self-reflective, and attuned to its own critical limitations; it engages and negotiates with the various horizons of specific doodles and doodlers, employing mixed methodologies – for example, biographical, historicist, formalist, materialist, and psychoanalytic – to understand them. Doodles speak with their perceivers in ways that require complex dialogic relationships, and this Element strives both to enact such relationships and to establish a framework for further scholarly interrogation and exploration. Recognising doodles as slippery subjects, this study also deploys some forms of post-structuralist and post-critical hermeneutics. Doodles themselves are rich with dialetheias: they are verbal and visual, squiggle and symbol, complete and incomplete, helpmeet and daemon. They require

[2] For a concise explanation of the concept of horizon in phenomenology and Gadamer's notion of the 'fusion of horizons', see Lawn and Keane 2011, 51–53.

complex methodologies for interpretation but also entice scholars to embrace them as evidence of other forms of reading, writing, and pleasure.

Ultimately, this Element recommends a more active, playful, and to some degree subjective interpretive approach than literary scholarship typically embodies, not only because doodles demand such an approach but also because doodling reminds us that meaning is always tentative, fragile, and relational. It unveils the pretence of objectivity that still garbs much criticism. It rejuvenates the joy and wonder of readerly discovery. Of course, there are dangers in this as well: doodles could become reduced to Rorschach tests, reflecting only the critic's preconceptions, or they could become unmoored from their original contexts and drift in a sea of overinterpretation. Yet here doodles also have surprising defence mechanisms – their difficulty and their embarrassing nature. Their contextual complexity (psychological, social, material, visual, etc.) resists easy interpretation and hence accentuates the ridiculousness of blithe attempts to assign unambiguous meaning to them such as Michael Watts's *Doodle Interpretation: A Beginner's Guide* (2000), in which he asserts, for example, that doodles of 'hearts that are sharply pointed at the base' indicate 'a highly judgemental person with a jealous streak' (17). Meanwhile, doodles' seeming silliness and inconsequential levity embarrass critics who take themselves and their theories too seriously, and so these critics tend to avoid doodles altogether. The most fruitful doodle criticism will thus be one that maintains a stance of fallibilistic play, aware of its own limitations and shortcomings but not afraid to risk looking foolish while playing with doodles. It will also play with all of the toys in the critical toy chest, trying out any lens that might unlock a new insight but handling these methodologies lightly, not becoming beholden or self-serious about any one approach.

In this Element, we have focused our attention on anglophone authors of the long nineteenth century, although doodling is present across many literary and linguistic cultures. We have done so not only because that is where our own scholarly expertise lies but also because it is the period during which industrial, commercial, literary, and artistic trends seeded the ground for the modern manifestation of doodling that would acquire its name in the early twentieth century. This era also featured ongoing and earnest debate about the role of levity in culture and education, making it an unsurprising time for doodling to appear in various contexts. Striving to be taken seriously at this time and beyond, women authors could not embrace doodling to the same degree as their male counterparts, and our study consequently draws on examples from primarily male authors; nonetheless, the doodling of the Brontës, Stevie Smith, and other authors provides rich counterexamples to this general trend.

We argue the case for the uniqueness of the long nineteenth century as a kind of golden age of doodling more fully in our forthcoming monograph on *Literary Doodling in Britain*, *1789–1930*, in which we trace the longer history of doodling and its development through technological, cultural, and aesthetic shifts across human civilisation. This first Element thus explores the various definitions of doodling (especially in the context of literary production and reception) and tries to draw generic boundaries between it and related artistic-literary forms such as sketching, caricaturing, illustrating, nonsense, and the grotesque. It further investigates literary doodling from a functional perspective, considering it as a transgeneric impulse or mode, theorising its relationship to other texts and activities, and emphasising its status as a spectral, liminal, and ludic form. This more synchronic approach is complemented by the more diachronic approach of our subsequent Element, where we show how the impulse to doodle has been a constant companion to the literary imagination even as its forms, functions, and materials have changed over time.

By taking literary doodling seriously, yet still playfully, as a subject of scholarly inquiry, this two-Element project aims to open various avenues for approaching doodles that others can follow and further refine, to highlight the interpenetration of the verbal and the visual in the imagination, and to expand our understanding of the creative process. It is an invitation to look beyond the polish of the published page and to enter the unruly yet playfully revealing realm of literary doodles.

DEMARCATION

1 Definitions

As the introduction argued, doodling is an important but relatively neglected aspect of writing and reading. But what precisely are doodles? And how does literary doodling differ from its more general practice? The introduction partially and implicitly described some of its traits, noting not only doodles' triviality and ambiguity but also their generative capacity. Although hard to decipher, doodles are nonetheless fascinating by-products of the tension between work and play; in the context of authors' doodling, they are indeterminate yet tantalising signals from the noise of literary creation. But what exact kind of artistic or literary phenomenon do they represent, and do they share any formal traits that would allow one consistently to recognise or classify them? How do they fit within a larger taxonomy of drawing and writing?

Starting deductively, one might turn to the *Oxford English Dictionary*'s (*OED*) definition: 'An aimless scrawl made by a person while his mind is more or less otherwise applied.' This description highlights doodles' key attributes of *purposelessness* and *distraction*. The *OED* furthermore defines 'scrawl' as a 'hastily and badly written letter' or 'a careless sketch', adding *haste*, *carelessness*, and *sloppiness* to the doodle's formal traits. In this definition, scrawl is also ambiguously lexical or pictorial (letter or sketch), transferring a similar irresolution between the verbal and visual onto the doodle. Can one apply these criteria – accepting them at least tentatively – to examples of potential doodles to distinguish them from graphically similar forms?

A quick comparison of two sets of drawings that ostensibly share these attributes reveals the limitations of the *OED*'s definition. Oscar Wilde's doodles (Figure 1) on MS p. 116 of his holograph notebook – undated but containing, among other things, drafts for *Poems* (1881) – seemingly possess the traits of roughness, hastiness, imprecision, or incompleteness that define scrawls. This autograph notebook page includes an abstract ornament in the upper right-hand corner, a very lightly sketched profile of a man wearing a monocle, and sketches of two additional figures – at least one of which sports a tonsure or cap – completed in a heavier line than the other sketch. Compared with the formal sketches of a Renaissance master such as

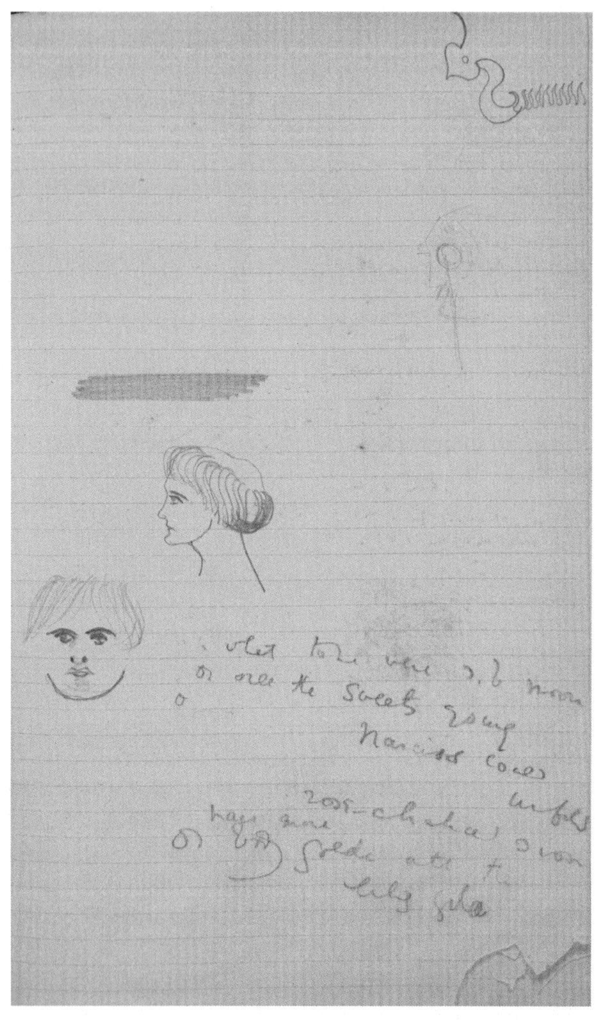

Figure 1 Oscar Wilde, 'Autograph manuscript of many poems, in a notebook illustrated with numerous sketches' (*c.* 1880). Free Library of Philadelphia, rbl0000146, MS page 116/140. Image courtesy of the Free Library of Philadelphia, Rare Book Department. Reproduced with kind permission of Merlin Holland. © *Estate of Oscar Wilde*.

Figure 2 Leonardo da Vinci, *Studies of the Heads of Two Warriors* (*c.* 1505). Museum of Fine Arts, Budapest. Public Domain.

Leonardo or, for that matter, any deliberate drawings by a draughtsman or woman with atelier training, these pencil drawings seem imprecise or incomplete; they are fairly minimalistic line drawings as opposed to careful figurative studies with detailed shading and nuanced perspective. Yet one could describe even a work such as Leonardo's *Studies of the Heads of Two Warriors* (*c.* 1505) as in some ways incomplete. This chalk drawing (Figure 2) – a preparatory sketch for Leonardo's planned fresco *The Battle of Anghiari* (1505) – is a *modello*, a life drawing that represents an intermediate stage between final fresco and the most preliminary sketch, the *primo pensiero* (first thought) or *schizzo* (quick sketch) (Culotta 2021).

Despite the exquisitely detailed expressions of the two figures, one profile sketch is more sparsely drawn than the other, and both trail off beyond the highly refined face and neck into greater abstraction. The visible construction lines reveal the method of making 'slight sketches' for which Leonardo advocated in *A Treatise on Painting*. Nevertheless, Leonardo's drawing could hardly be described as an aimless scrawl; it is self-evidently the product of intense concentration and long deliberation – what he called *discorso mentale* (Capra 2013, 3) – and represents a careful study of the figures' dramatic and somewhat grotesque expressions. The more cursory details are deliberately underdeveloped, allowing the focus of the work to be on the precise and meticulous delineation of the faces and providing space for further additions (e.g., hats and helmets) to the finalised fresco.

Leonardo's drawing demonstrates the importance of context and purpose to the classification of doodles. Although Wilde's simple outline sketches appear less refined than Leonardo's, Wilde created the former in a very different context: that of the writer's notebook, which Howard Junker (1995) describes as 'uncertain, ungainly, unliterary'; 'only scribbling' (1). Writers' notebooks are multi-generic, gestational, and (semi-)private; they are a 'compendious literary form' marked by raw content that is 'uncooked sometimes to the point of illegibility' (2–3). As such, one cannot apply benchmarks of completeness and precision to their contents in the same way – at least not without a highly relative and subjective contextual understanding of that content. The truth of this observation is evident when applied to even Leonardo's notebooks, which contain drawings much more raw, indeterminate, playful, and experimental than his more formal sketches. (See Figure 3.) Not only are Wilde's doodles situated in a private and more gestational context, but they are also rendered in a style visually more consistent with the outline drawings of nineteenth-century illustration or caricature than with Italian Renaissance draughtsmanship. The drawings' precision and completeness – their apparent sparseness – are thus factors of those genres' conventions rather than the standards to which Leonardo worked or to some decontextualised measure of virtuosity. The style of Wilde's drawing is also not the result of any artistic limitation. Although less renowned a draughtsman than Leonardo, Wilde was nonetheless a skilled amateur artist, winning multiple school prizes for his drawing (Sturgis 2018, 23, 27). While Wilde's doodles do not by themselves suggest the work of

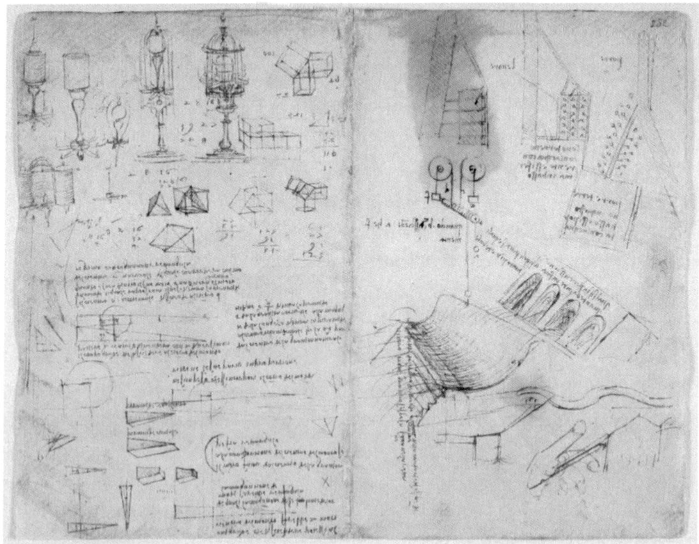

Figure 3 Leonardo da Vinci, notebook ('The Codex Arundel'), early sixteenth century. British Library, Arundel MS 263, ff. 283v, 282. Public domain. Used with permission of the British Library.

a master draughtsman, this biographical knowledge and Wilde's general facility with a pencil leave little doubt that Wilde, had he chosen to, might have created more detailed and complete drawings.

The determination of whether a drawing is a scrawl or not thus depends at least partially on biographical or other contextual information. Even with such information, one needs further details about the scrawls to identify them as doodles. According to the *OED*'s definition, doodles are not just scrawls but aimless scrawls. Absent direct commentary from Wilde on his doodling, one must employ close reading to attempt to understand Wilde's purpose. Yet a close reading of the images provides little indication of their purpose, completeness, or level of precision. The page itself (MS p. 116) lacks an obvious centre of authorial or readerly focus and is divided into at least four or five discrete areas of activity with no clear relationship to each other: four drawings and a draft stanza of the poem 'La Belle Gabrielle'.[3] The drawing in the top corner of the page is a classic abstract design one idly makes while distracted, a playing with shapes and patterns more in line with Leonardo's *ludi geometrici* than with his formal sketches. Wilde's profile sketches also lack an implicit purpose or any clear relationship to the accompanying text. Located among Wilde's manuscript drafts of *Poems*, these drawings, one would assume, illustrate or at least relate in some oblique way to Wilde's verses; however, there is no discernible relationship except collocation between the drawings and 'La Belle Gabrielle', a poem that deploys various classical myths of unrequited or auto-erotic love, including allusions to Narcissus, Salmacis, and Endymion. There is nothing about the figurative drawings to suggest their definite association with these myths or other details of the poem. At most one might detect a tenuous connection between the more lightly sketched profile (Figure 4) – whose monocle could suggest a caricature of James McNeill Whistler (1834–1903) – and the draft of 'In the Gold Room. A Harmony', the poem with the Whistleresque title situated on the pages before and after MS p. 116. But this relationship – should it even exist – is not one of illustration but of loose association. It is the kind of relationship one often sees with doodling: the daydream and its tenuous connection to the activity from which it is an escape.

Wilde's drawings lack a self-evident purpose. They are digressions from the adjacent verse and the larger notebook manuscript. In this sense, Wilde's drawings start to satisfy one criterion of the *OED*'s definition – that is, Wilde made the drawings while his mind was 'more or less otherwise applied'. The drawings are seemingly purposeless distractions from Wilde's main activity of literary composition. Applied to the examples of Leonardo's and Wilde's drawings, the *OED* definition has thus

[3] 'La Belle Gabrielle' (as transcribed from the notebook with interpolations borrowed from Wilde 2000, 92–93): 'Ah what to me were s.b. <silver-breasted> moon / Or all the sweets young Narciss could unfold / <Or wondering lovers, or> rose-chaliced swoon / Or hair [***] made golde with the lily<'s> gold.' The poem was unpublished in Wilde's lifetime.

Figure 4 Oscar Wilde, 'Autograph manuscript of many poems, in a notebook illustrated with numerous sketches' (*c*. 1880). Free Library of Philadelphia, rbl0000146, MS page 116/140 (detail). Image courtesy of the Free Library of Philadelphia, Rare Book Department. Reproduced with kind permission of Merlin Holland. © *Estate of Oscar Wilde*.

revealed some limitations but also suggested that doodles minimally lack a discernible purpose or at least possess a significantly divergent purpose from concomitant activities or texts. This definition also underscores that one cannot identify doodles in isolation. Context matters. Doodles must be defined against some other activity, and the relationship between them and that activity is often desultory and sometimes antagonistic. The relational aspect of doodling is what distinguishes it in modern parlance from scribbling, for which the *OED* uses similar adjectives – quick, careless, irregular, 'apparently meaningless' – but without suggesting that scribbling has any necessary relationship to another activity. In contrast, doodles frequently emerge from the productive tension between work and play. Doodles are distractions from lectures, assignments, chores, or jobs – particularly ones for which writing and drawing implements are already employed. For instance, see the four centuries of doodles in ledgers owned by the Banco di Napoli archive and reproduced in Zevola (1993). In the case of *literary doodling*, they are typically examples of authors' distractedness. Like everyone else, literary authors are prone to inattention or daydreaming; they are similarly inspired to doodle while listening to lectures, reading, or engaged in some other activity whether painful or pleasurable. Frequently literary doodles are also divergent products of specific professional writing activities: composing, reading, ideating, and note taking. In any of these scenarios, doodling can be a window into the author's mind, although doodles are also at least partially spontaneous, involuntary, or subconscious. They are not simply consciously constructed text (e.g., a set of deliberate annotations) sitting alongside another work within the space of the same page. They are ruptures from and within that parallel activity. That is also why they appear coarse and incomplete: they burst forth from a set of constraints and are marked by that effort.

The dictionary definition of doodling has been a somewhat useful but incomplete starting point for demarcating this phenomenon. The *OED*'s characterisation of scrawl, which undergirds its definition of doodle, highlights superficial traits that are insufficient to differentiate doodles from other, visually similar genres like the graffito, sketch, reader's mark, cartoon, caricature, or illustration. Defining doodles more precisely and understanding their role in the formation and reception of literary works requires both further analysis and engagement with theorical conceptions of doodling, such as they exist. The meaning of words is always 'much subtler, fuzzier, and messier' than one assumes, and lexicography aims 'not to classify objects in the world' but 'to summarize . . . the conventional meaning a word has in a language' (Hanks 2015, 112–13). This conventional meaning in 'natural language' cannot, as Patrick Hanks argues, 'be defined by stipulating necessary and sufficient conditions for set membership'

(113) – that is, the dictionary definition cannot serve as a comprehensive rubric to evaluate potential doodles for membership in that class.

As opposed to lexicography, genre theory provides an approach that can establish these conditions for membership, offering a way to determine the forms and boundaries of an artistic or literary genre. Of course, genre theory itself is a notoriously fraught site of evolving elucidation and debate exemplified by the work of leading twentieth-century formalist or structuralist critics such as Mikhail Bakhtin, Northrop Frye, Tzvetan Todorov, and Gérard Genette. At its core, though, genre theory recognises, as John Frow (2015) asserts, that genre is a 'set of conventional and highly organised constraints on the production and interpretation of meaning' (10). Todorov (1990) states Frow's point more directly: 'literary genres . . . are nothing but . . . choices among discursive possibilities, choices that a given society has made conventional' (10). Borrowing categories from the semiotician Charles Morris, Todorov locates 'discursive properties' of any text on multiple levels of discourse: 'semantic', 'syntactic', or 'verbal' (18). (See also Morris 1971.) In other words, these properties can relate to a text's *meaning*, *structure*, or *presentation*. But doodles resist the easy application of these taxonomic strategies. As a kind of writing or drawing that is at least partially subconscious – especially for those artists working before the wide dissemination of the concept – doodling is less apt to represent a creator's conscious utilisation of formal constraints than other genres. Setting aside questions of intentionality and focusing on the meaning of the doodles themselves, readers and scholars are still thwarted in their efforts. Doodles are not just semiconscious creations; they are also visual and verbal inventions that frequently have no discernible meaning. Doodles tend to derive whatever meaning they possess from their oft-nebulous relationships with another text or activity. Doodling is a distracted enterprise that might reveal – through an investigation of paratactic relationships, the application of psychoanalysis, or other methods – meaningful relationships between doodles and the activities from which they depart. But both the presence and recovery of that meaning are never guaranteed. Must one then exclude all doodles whose meaning is at best opaque in order to define the doodle as a traditional genre? And how accurate would that definition then be? Conversely, might opacity itself embody the genre's central attribute? In that case there is little hope for a systematic scholarly exploration of the subject.

Doodles' semantic opacity challenges the critic who wants to define doodling as a genre based on its denotative value (its meaning). Doodles' syntactic aspect – the 'relation of the parts among themselves' (Todorov 1990, 18) – is also unlikely to help one define the genre. Most doodles are either singular symbols or otherwise situated within a constellation of doodles whose meaning is equally obscure. The meaning of one part of a doodle, let alone its relationship to other parts, is likely to be as opaque as the meaning of the entire doodle. The last aspect, the verbal – 'everything connected with the material manifestations of the signs themselves' (18) – has more potential.[4] Doodles might be roughly drawn or scribbled; they might be nonsensical or abstract, opaque or bizarre, but they possess a material presence on the page, one that could theoretically be broken down and codified in the service of defining the genre. But doodles' physical aspects alone are insufficient for distinguishing them from other types of whimsical or incomplete writing/drawing such as the sketch or caricature. Even highly formal works of art such as the paintings of Joan Miró or Cy Twombly can purposefully mimic the simple lines and seemingly unsophisticated designs of doodles.

The fact that artists like Twombly can mimic the doodle's traits – and have that mimicry be meaningful to an audience – suggests that there is still another way to define doodles as a genre. By first exploring critical discourses about doodling, we can pinpoint the unique set of traits that might describe the doodle as a genre. Todorov cautions that the key to defining genre lies not in simply finding a common trait among members of a potential class. Acknowledging that one can almost always identify a common property between two texts – and thus create an artificial class – Todorov seeks to limit genre to 'classes of texts that have been historically perceived as such' (17). Our efforts thus far to establish the doodle as a genre by identifying its unique attributes risk the creation of an arbitrary class. As Todorov's argument

[4] Todorov replaces Morris's third term, 'pragmatics' – the relationship between signs and their interpreters – with 'verbal'. For the definition of pragmatics, see Morris 1971, 43–54.

suggests, we should instead invert our investigation and first establish an historical recognition of the doodle as a genre.

Without limiting genres to their analyses, Todorov nevertheless shifts the critic's focus away from textual features onto 'metadiscursive discourse' and self-reflective discourse in 'literary texts themselves' (17). That is, he recentres the effort to identify any particular genre on its presence within critical discourse *about* genres as well as in any discussion – implied or explicit – *within* texts about the genres that they inhabit. Although a work of art rather than criticism, Twombly's *Fifty Days at Iliam* (1978) is a good example of the latter category; it is a pictorial work in which self-reflective discourse about doodling – the painting's implied allusions to the form – reveals that the genre is well understood by its audience. The apparent genre to which Twombly's painting alludes, however, is not necessarily one established by scholars. Nearly everyone doodles, a fact that suggests the existence of a concomitant, albeit relatively unsophisticated, popular discourse/practice into which Twombly's painting taps. The countless mass-market books published on the subject reinforce this supposition. Yet works like Twombly's painting and the popular wisdom from which it draws provide a shaky foundation on which to build a precise typology. While these discussions reveal the historical presence of the doodle as a genre, they depend more on a 'sight-test' (of the 'you know it when you see it' variety) than on a precise delineation of the genre's traits.

Far outnumbered by popular discussions, a small canon of scholarly treatises on doodling exists.[5] Despite the ambiguity of most doodles, these critical works tend to offer precise accountings of the genre's formal attributes. In other words, they take seriously Todorov's caveat that genres cannot be reduced to metadiscourse alone and must retain their discursive function – that is, their descriptive power. He argues that the 'study of genres . . . must have as its ultimate objective precisely the establishment of these [concrete] properties' common to any class of texts (17). In short, common traits among texts do not establish a class; metadiscourse about genres does. But that metadiscourse must still identify a genre's common

[5] And there is a growing interest in the subject, especially among more recently established and emerging scholars. For example, see Marangoni 2013 and Dickson 2022.

traits. Although individually clear about the genre's concrete attributes, these scholars do not always agree among themselves. Nonetheless, an examination of metadiscursive discourse on doodling, supplemented by popular definitions, is a propitious starting point for one to establish the reality of doodling as a genre and to begin to delineate its formal parameters.

The first extensive examination of doodles – and the source of one of the *OED*'s earliest quotations in which the word appears – is Russell M. Arundel's *Everybody's Pixillated: A Book of Doodles* (1937). In many ways the urtext of doodle criticism, this book is one with which many subsequent scholars have begun their investigations. Arundel's book itself draws from Frank Capra's film *Mr. Deeds Comes to Town* (1936), to which the title alludes and in which the eponymous character, played by Gary Cooper, explains that doodling is the activity in which people 'make foolish designs on paper while they're thinking'. Capra's film is a comedy, and Arundel's book is itself only a semi-serious exploration of the phenomenon that Mr. Deeds defines. As Arundel explains, he treats his subject with a 'touch of the serious' only 'here and there', but his definition of doodles has been influential: 'a scribbling or sketch made while the conscious mind is concerned with matters wholly unrelated to the scribbling' (ix). Our exploration in this Element seeks to understand doodling in a literary context in a way that includes but goes beyond the parameters of aimlessness and distractedness that Arundel establishes. His understanding of doodling nevertheless remains essential to most subsequent explorations of the term. *Everybody's Pixillated* not only offers this essential definition of doodling but also seeks, without trepidation, to enumerate the genre's formal attributes, going so far as to include a 'pixillation chart' (Figure 5). This chart both attempts to codify the various forms of doodles and seeks to provide psychological explanations for each type. Arundel explicitly attempts to advertise doodle-reading as a form of popular psychoanalysis derived from the then-serious use of doodles by 'psychiatrists' seeking 'accurate pictures of the Subconscious Mind' (x). Capitalising on doodling's prominence in Capra's film, in which the act of doodling is a sign of 'pixillation' or insanity, Arundel's chart offers his readers a method of

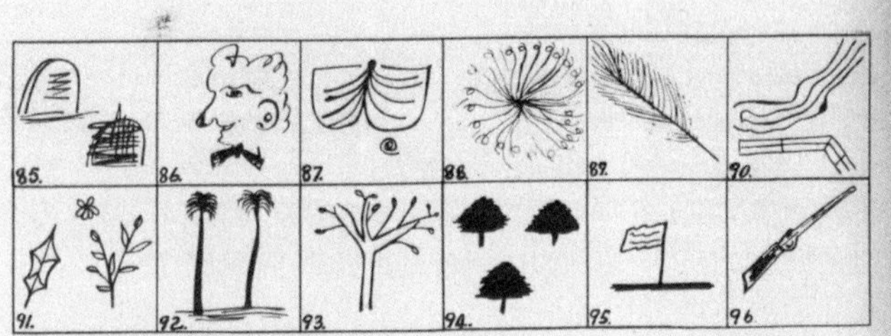

85. You have a solemn nature, and a morbid fear of death. Probably timid.

86. This pattern has many exaggerated features. You are inclined to exaggeration, but have a sense of humor which offsets this imperfection.

87. You have a fear of high places, and feel a strange urge to move into space when near a window or a high building. You are suffering from hypsophobia. (This pattern starts at top and is built outward and downward.)

88. Very fine, wavy and close-packed lines. You are a dreamer and idealist. An æsthetic nature.

89. You are quiet, shy, sentimental and romantic.

90. You are a daydreamer with a practical love of travel.

91. If female, you are pleasantly feminine and well-balanced. If male, you are fond of the outdoors. Probably fond of animals and flowers.

92. Romantic. Sentimental. Probably a very lonely person.

93. Strong sex desire or fixation.

94. You are very fond of outdoors. A lover of nature.

95. (One simple design standing alone.) You are easily depressed and cannot stand being alone. Inclined to melancholia.

96. You have a fundamental fear of guns, possibly as the result of a bad experience with them.

80

Figure 5 Russell M. Arundel, *Everybody's Pixillated: A Book of Doodles* (1937), page 80.

analysing their own doodles. The author warns us, though, that the chart is 'not held to be infallible' (71).

Despite his exhaustive typology of doodles, Arundel sets for himself a seemingly impossible task: carefully to describe and classify a kingdom of ineffable and decontextualised squiggles. The futility of his effort is revealed in a series of caveats Arundel provides to his readers. Quoting a Dr I. Silverman of Gallinger Hospital, he first cautions that:

> There is no code by which these subconscious sketches may be interpreted, as each symbol is individual to the artist, and for anyone else to attempt to explain would be presumptuous. The only accurate interpretation must be furnished by the artist himself, and then only through some psychoanalytic technique. (Quoted in Arundel 1937, 71)

Somewhat paradoxically, only doodlers 'know' the meaning of their work, but not without a psychoanalyst's aid. Next, Arundel warns that the content or 'pattern' of the doodle is less important than the '*manner or style* in which the doodle is made' (72) (emphasis original). For example, lines that are 'heavy', 'even', or 'wavy' offer clues to various psychological states, but one assumes that this interpretive approach could apply equally to handwriting or drawing of any sort (72). Lastly, and perhaps most rationally, Arundel reiterates his admonition about the fallibility of his book by questioning his readers' sanity: 'If the chart doesn't happen to tell the truth, just remember the foreword – "This is a pixillated book for pixillated people"' (72).

Arundel's three caveats succinctly summarise the paradoxes that have vexed doodles studies since his book's publication. On one hand, we feel intuitively that doodles mean *something*; on the other hand, we neither know what they mean nor how exactly to determine it. Ultimately unsuccessful as an interpretive endeavour, Arundel is at least undaunted by these inherent challenges and attempts to decode doodles through the use of his 'pixillation chart', by means of which he detects 'one hundred and twenty patterns which most often appear in doodles' (72). This chart empowers him to offer unequivocal interpretations of specific doodles – largely those of celebrities – based solely on an analysis of their style.

For example, he examines a set of scribbles by Kentucky senator Marvel Mills Logan (1874–1939) and asserts that the doodling 'unmistakably indicates a deep-seated sense of humor and a methodical mind' (20). In light of Arundel's previous assertion that the individuality of doodles means that 'no code' can unlock their meaning, one cannot take his readings too seriously. Instead we must see his text as a work of 'good humor', not the exhaustive and careful description of the form that it appears to be (ix). Despite falling short of its taxonomic aims, *Everybody's Pixillated* is nevertheless important. It not only initiates critical discussion of the doodle as a genre, but it also collates a corpus of doodles created during the roughly 150 years before the book's publication, a corpus demonstrating that the phenomenon predates its christening.

Very little serious critical analysis of doodles appeared after Arundel's book – if one can even apply that adjective to his effort – until E. H. Gombrich addressed the subject in his introduction to a collection of doodles drawn from historical bank ledgers (1991; reprinted and translated in Gombrich 1999).[6] Gombrich (1999) defines doodles as an expression of human beings' 'play instinct', one that engages both writing and 'image-making' (213). In line with the *OED*'s and Arundel's definitions, his study further notes that doodling typically takes place while the doodler is bored or 'in a state of distracted attention' (222). Distraction is thus central to all three of these definitions. Gombrich's work moves beyond earlier explorations, though, by demarcating more concretely the boundaries between doodles and related genres. Namely, he contrasts doodles with graffiti and other public art forms. Identifying doodles as the 'less innocent brother[s] of the graffito', he argues that the doodler 'normally wishes [for his work] to remain private', while the graffiti artist is 'tempted to disfigure a white wall . . . mainly to exercise power and get rid of his aggression'

6 Helen King's (1957) *Your Doodles and What They Mean to You* is one semi-serious interlude similar to Arundel's book. Like *Everybody's Pixillated*, King's book offers a typology of doodles in the form of her 'doodle dictionary', of which David Maclagan (2014) notes: 'it is remarkable how little overlap there is' between King's dictionary and Arundel's pixillation chart (56).

(225). This distinction helps to explain why graffitists choose as their canvases prominent public locations – walls, trains, bathroom stalls – while doodlers practise in notebooks, manuscripts, and printed books. Gombrich's analysis is an important attempt to classify doodles as a distinct genre, one that takes an approach of comparing and contrasting genres that this Element employs in the next sections. However, his methods rely partly on intentionality – the doodler's purpose (aimless play or serious effort), desire (privacy or publicity), and state of mind (distraction or boredom) – and consequently present ongoing complications for classification.

Most subsequent academic and semi-scholarly uses of the term *doodling* reinforce the basic definition evoked in Gombrich's discussion but also introduce conflicting criteria. Writing in *The American Scholar*, Matthew Battles (2004) emphatically underscores doodles' lack of intentionality. On these grounds, he distinguishes doodles from scribbles, glosses, marginalia, rubrications, sketches, graffiti, and the marks of printers, authors, and readers. Arguing that 'scribbling is not doodling' because the former is executed 'in haste or by an uncertain hand', he asserts that the latter is 'beyond craft and criticism' (107). Unlike the 'preliminary brainstorming of sketching and the territorial mark-making of graffiti', doodling is, according to Battles, the 'graphic expression of ennui' (107). Using the example of Ralph Waldo Emerson's juvenile doodling, of which he argues 'little can be said', Battles concludes that doodling is not only purposeless but also incomprehensible (108). From this position, he excludes from his definition the marks of readers, writers, printers, and editors for their intentionality and asserts that '[i]f a doodle has anything to tell us about the creative work of its author, then it isn't a doodle' (108). Battles's essay reinforces the emphasis on non-intentionality in doodle scholarship. Moreover, it extends Gombrich's boundary-drawing to include numerous related genres. The essay also points out a categorical mistake in the definitions that this Element previously explored: namely, that haste or imprecision are concepts improperly applied to doodles, which exist outside categories of refinement and skill. However, Battles's definition too easily dismisses doodling's semantic (and counter-semantic) potential – perhaps in part because his exemplar, Emerson, purged doodles from his journals as he aged (consequently suggesting a trajectory from pre-symbolic gesture to verbal articulation), but primarily because he does not address doodles' oblique, latent, or paratactical meanings.

Battles's definition sharpens our generic focus through boundary-drawing, but his insistence on doodles' unintelligibility puts him at odds with Arundel, Gombrich, and other critics who see at least some interpretive potential in exploring writers' and readers' doodles. One such critic is David Maclagan (2014), who, like Battles, argues that scribbles are not doodles, although he sees both (alongside 'automatic drawing') as lying on a 'spectrum of involuntary or absent-minded mark-making' (29). He defines scribbling as a genre or category of mark-making that acquired in response to developments in modernist art the connotation of a deliberately spontaneous (however paradoxical) and counter-signifying activity, a negation or cancellation of meaning. Before the twentieth century, Maclagan notes, the term was more expansive, serving as a blanket term for 'the most elementary scrawls as well as more complex non-representational drawings that did not fit into established pigeonholes' (10). As scribbling takes on a narrower meaning in the twentieth century, doodling comes to embody some of the early connotations of scribbling, including 'spontaneous and absent-minded' drawing (57). Maclagan distinguishes the modern categories of scribble and doodle, then, by defining the former as having no 'semiotics' – it 'erases messages' – while the latter 'are seen as carrying messages' that, even if implicit, 'are capable of being deciphered' (21).

Yet another scholar, David Prescott-Steed (2010), defines doodling as a form of radical freedom that is neither aimless nor meaningless. He agrees with Maclagan that doodles are decipherable, but not because they have an inherent meaning accessible to any audience. Instead, he argues that doodling is '"asemic" writing' that readers nonetheless make meaningful through subjective analysis (n.p.). Doodles are expressive but only through the hard labour of interpretation absent conventional frameworks. Prescott-Stead admits that doodling can be 'simply about spending time, wasting time, and passing time', but in its most radical forms it 'facilitates a new relationship with meaning (that is, with the limits of meaning)' (n.p.). Whereas writing conventions enable and make efficient communication, planning, and remembering, doodling exposes the limitations of those conventions and reveals new vistas through an adversarial relationship with traditional writing. While not denying that distraction can be an element of doodling, Prescott-Stead shifts our understanding of its function from structuralist semiotics to post-structuralist play.

In addition to these general investigations of doodling are some important explications of the work of individual doodlers. Focusing on the work of specific writer-artists, these scholars tend to offer less comprehensive definitions, but they also contradict Battles's characterisation of doodling as non-expressive. For example, in Stevie Smith's doodles – as she herself called them – William May finds an 'unconscious artistic impulse', the products of which Smith subsequently curated and refined in an effort to expand the range of interpretative possibilities inherent in her writing (May 2010, 182). Smith was not a trained artist, but she enjoyed doodling, the results of which often delighted her: 'sometimes the dogs which come have such a look in their eyes that you can't believe that you've done them. And the faces that come!' (quoted in May 2010, 182). Like other doodles, Smith's drawings are 'messy, anomalous, unfinished, and accidental', yet the faces that she sketches are richly expressive (173). One wonders whether Smith is not purposefully invoking Rodolphe Töpffer, often credited with being a founder of modern comics, who advises in his *Essay on Physiognomy* ((1845) 1965) that anyone can:

> acquire – alone, with no help except what he gets by thousands of tries – all he needs to know about physiognomy in order to produce expressive faces whenever he likes – wretched in drawing, maybe, but definite and unmistakable in their meaning. (11)

Smith's description of her doodling process demonstrates one way in which doodles can be subconscious creations whose meaning is still 'definite and unmistakable' in Töpffer's words.

Moreover, as May argues, Smith strategically deploys her doodles as agents in the larger semiotic networks constructed from the intersections of her writing, her drawing, and the space of the page. By juxtaposing word and image or by deliberately refining her drawings, Smith imbues her doodles with meaning. In an interview with Jonathan Williams, she explains the latter process, making a generic distinction between doodles and other drawings: 'If I suddenly get caught by the doodle, I put more effort into it and end up calling it a drawing' (Smith 1974, 113). Yet by refashioning doodles into drawings, she does not detract from their initial aimlessness; in fact, their 'anarchic' and 'pre-verbal' genesis creates the semantically disruptive force that Smith intends (May 2010, 172). Although Smith's process highlights a somewhat idiosyncratic method by which doodles can acquire greater expressive certainty, it adds to the metadiscourse on doodling and opens up new channels – contextual and genetic – for interpretation.

Like May, Jean Paul Riquelme (2013) explores the implications of a single author's doodling, in this case Oscar Wilde's alphabetical doodling from an early manuscript fragment of his play *An Ideal Husband* (1893) and later interpolations that Wilde made to the acting script as he prepared page proofs for the published edition of 1899. With respect to the draft, Riquelme focuses on one particular scribbling at the top of a manuscript page: a playful, vertical rewriting of the word *IDEAL* in which the letters intersect and overlap in a way reminiscent of concrete poetry and which Riquelme calls an 'anagrammatical drawing' or an 'anadoodlegram' (292). (The letters I, D, and A are superimposed on each other in a way that also creates the letter R.) Riquelme is interested in this figure for what it suggests about Wilde's 'exuberant' writing process, marked in his words by an 'aleatoric exfoliation of signifiers and a carnivalising interpolation of diverse figures and perspectives' (289). He draws out from Wilde's pictogram a combination of letters that spell words with thematic importance throughout the play – *ideal*, *idle*, *lied*, *real*, *leader*, *lie*, and *die* (of which Wilde created a sketch) – and makes an argument about the generative nature of this orthographic drawing and the role it might have played in Wilde's compositional process.

Riquelme's description of the anadoodlegram is an apt one for literary doodling in general. He sees Wilde's drawing as 'integral' to his writing and identifies this particular anagrammatic drawing as a 'kind of alphabetical linear origami that can be reconfigured into various linguistic shapes' (294). Like those of other scholars, Riquelme's definition of doodles centres on traits that this Element finds fundamental to the genre: graphic and semantic free play, potential non-signification or multi-vocal expression, confusion between the visual and verbal. However, Riquelme makes a distinction between sketches (e.g., of 'heads and objects') and the 'occasional doodle – not a representation of an object or a person but seemingly idle scribbling or a drawing of one or more letters or letterlike shapes' (294). While not eschewing the sketches and other figurative drawings all together – for example, he does offer some speculative comments about the drawing of the die and how it might suggest 'lie' and 'chance' (296) – Riquelme nonetheless falls back on familiar modes of literary criticism that privilege the linguistic aspects of writing and separate them from accompanying pictorial content, implying a categorical distinction between the symbolic (alphabetic and linguistic) *doodle* – related to *scribble* – and the merely representational (albeit potentially suggestive) *sketch*. Undoubtedly, Riquelme uses signification to delineate the boundaries between doodles and sketches in large part because the act of extracting meaning from the pictorial doodle is so much more difficult and much less certain than exploring the relationship between a word or series of words and an entire literary text. Nonetheless, sketches such as those in the early manuscript of *An Ideal Husband* share the traits that Riquelme ascribes to Wilde's anadoodlegram and must be accounted for in any holistic theory of literary doodling.

Having witnessed the diversity of metadiscursive opinions, one is tempted to argue that doodles are defined only by their lack of a singular definition. However, the key concepts undergirding doodling – if not the doodle's formal traits – arise clearly from these discussions. Regardless of emphasis, the definitions of each author discussed herein engage with the concepts of *intentionality*, *playfulness*, *completeness*, *signification* (or *non-signification*), and *word–image relationships*.[7] Sometimes contradictory, these definitions nonetheless reveal that there is more to doodles than aimlessness and distraction. Any comprehensive definition with utility for scholars must therefore account for all of these listed concepts, while also attempting to reconcile or at least explain the conflicting definitions among scholars.

[7] Whether these relationships appear internally within the doodle itself – as in Riquelme's anadoodlegram – or externally between the doodle and another text.

One way that this Element proposes to harmonise these incongruities is to distinguish between what Todorov calls the *functional* and *structural* approaches to classification (2). The former approach allows one to understand doodles from the perspective of their function within 'a larger system' (2); that is, one can ask, à la Prescott-Stead and Riquelme, what doodles *do* within a larger context (e.g., the space of the page) as opposed to what they *are* or how they *appear*. Using this method, we can define as doodles phenomena not immediately recognisable as such – for example, Wilde's prose interpolations to the acting script of *An Ideal Husband*. Without understanding the function of these interpolations, one could not categorise them as doodles, although they are most accurately described as such. These inserted stage directions are playful interlocutions between paratext and text that confound and reshape rather than illuminate the play's meaning. They are doodles in the sense that their relationship to the text is *doodlistic* – that is, ludic, liminal, and spectral. As might be apparent, this explanation of doodling shifts the emphasis from formal attributes to effects and relationships, and it starts to engage with questions of *mode* in addition to genre. The key difference between mode and genre is that the former is transhistorical and trans-generic – a potentiality implicit in expression itself – while the latter is, as Frow (2015) describes, a set of 'specific and time-bound formal structures' (71). According to Frow, modes are extensions of genre beyond formal structures into 'broader specification[s] of "tone"' (71); one applies them adjectivally to describe traits originally derived from genres but divorced from their structural anchors. Examples include the adjectives in 'lyric drama', 'comic novel', and 'doodlistic illustration'.

By focusing on doodling as a mode, we can understand better how doodles function and escape some of the thornier questions about definition and genre with which we have grappled. We do this not to avoid these questions but because the doodle is a playful parasite, unique among genres in requiring a host text and potentially threatening that host's structural foundation. As the close readings that follow demonstrate, the structure of the doodle – its ineffable lines and cryptic messages – performs its simultaneously poly- and asemic function. Whereas Todorov (1990) argues that '[s]tructure and function do not imply each other in a rigorous way, even though it is always possible to observe affinities between them', doodles conflate form and function (2). Unlike sketches, for example, which always share with each other a set of recognisable visual or verbal traits, doodles share a function engendered by its formal features, but these are shapeshifting traits that arise in response to specific texts. And while the bulk of doodles look alike, their apparent similarity reveals a shared visual, yet largely subliminal vocabulary that doodlers deploy in idiosyncratic ways.

A doodle's structure cannot be separated from its function; however, the structure (and meaning) of doodles often escapes precise identification. Nevertheless, the doodle remains an historically defined genre, one whose features require explication. Luckily, the doodle's conflation of form and function imposes a method of understanding its nebulous structure. By revealing the function of a particular doodle, one can begin to discern the purpose of its structure and thereby start to codify a typical – though not absolute – set of concrete attributes, one that many observers will recognise intuitively. The structural approach also allows us more readily to assemble a set of formally related genres that we then deploy in order to draw the doodle's generic parameters. As Todorov (1990) argues, a generic norm 'becomes visible . . . owing only to its transgressions' (14). Consequently, this Element defines doodling not only through its (limited) scholarly discussion but also by testing the boundaries between doodles and related forms, comparing doodles (in the next sections) with sketches, caricatures, illustrations, and similar forms to ascertain whether doodling denotes an extra-generic activity, a subset of works within an established pictorial or literary genre, or a distinct category in its own right.

This Element argues that doodles are, indeed, a unique genre – one similar to, yet in important ways radically different from, other forms of writing or drawing. Doodling is a genre, but it is more than that. It is also a set of practices and effects – a mode or impulse – that influences the *genre* of doodling and pervades other forms (more on doodling as a mode in the Exploration part of this Element). And while these taxonomic efforts might seem esoteric or trivial, this Element argues that literary doodling is an important aspect of literary corpora more generally, and its study enables one to understand better the basic process of literary genesis as well as the general mental and corporeal farrago from which writing emerges. Additionally, criticism on doodling reveals the practices, habits, and intellectual preoccupations, conscious and subconscious, of specific authors. Lastly, and most important, the analysis of doodles reminds scholars of the destabilising yet productive contradictions and complexities of those individual minds, resituating literary genesis and reception in the minds – or at least their material traces – of authors and readers. Doodles trouble the meaning of texts and thereby (re)introduce semantic flexibility into literary works and their reception. A sketch or an illustration might reinforce the meaning of a text; however, a doodle might destabilise, explode, or at least complicate that meaning.

2 Sketches

Especially when they are figurative, pictorial doodles are often labelled as sketches in catalogues and critical analyses, so a juxtaposition of the two forms might bring the differences between them into greater relief. Sketches suggest, as Sunni Brown (2014) defines them, 'quick, unrefined drawing[s]' (12). That description certainly applies to most doodles and forms part of the definition(s) that we have already explored. Claude Marks (1972) similarly describes sketches, but with slightly less emphasis on their pictorial quality, as 'rapid spontaneous notations of ideas and impressions that might be jotted down in a sketchbook or on an odd sheet of paper for the benefit of the artist himself or his intimate friends' (1). The *OED*'s definition of sketch expands on both Brown's and Mark's, adding another layer to our understanding: a 'rough drawing or delineation of something, giving the outlines or prominent features without the detail, *esp[ecially]* one intended to serve as the basis of a more finished picture' (our emphasis). Thus, beyond their roughness and lack of detail, sketches often imply a stage of drawing along a continuum that leads from an artist's earliest sketches, the *primi pensieri*, to the work's final form.

We already see two distinct uses of the term *sketch*: a word for any rough or hastily executed drawing and a name for a rough or hasty drawing that is executed in preparation for another, more polished work. The first sense explains the term's widespread application to doodles, which are themselves typically unrefined and incomplete. These qualities also make sketches, as Martina Lauster (2007) describes them, 'ephemeral and seemingly amorphous' – another apt description of doodles (1). The second usage of the term, though, begins to delineate important differences between the two categories. Sketches and doodles can both mark various beginnings: the inception of drawings or works of literature within the space of private notebooks, sketchbooks, and manuscripts. But doodles are more bran than germ; they are present at the point of conception but do not evolve into the mature organism, although they might aid in its development. Whereas doodles imply no telos, no further refinement or goal, sketches are haunted by an essential absence: their graphic doppelgänger, the finished artwork. Sketches mark an early stage of conception. As Richard Sha (1998) explains, sketches emerge 'at the origins of the painter's invention process (the artist's first thoughts)' (4). Whether or not a sketch evolves into its consummate state, it remains defined by that realised or potential other.

In contrast to polished and exhibitory artworks, sketches are private and preparatory; nonetheless, they are marked by their creators' knowledge of that final, public form. This knowledge imbues sketches with a performative function. In one sense, this performance is a purposeful, yet still private experimentation with representation. In the late eighteenth and early nineteenth centuries, though, this performative aspect of sketching evolves into a formal genre in its own right and gives a third meaning to the word *sketch*. Concerned with naturalism, authenticity, and inspiration, artists of the Romantic era began to appropriate the sketch and to fashion from it a rhetoric of genuineness. As Sha (1998) argues, the sketch's '[h]asty brushwork and shading, broken lines, roughness, and irregularity' encourage viewers to imagine the 'spontaneous and authentic feelings' of the artist or the 'naturalistic and dynamic rendering of the landscape' (4). For eighteenth- and nineteenth-century audiences, the crudeness of sketches signified truth and immediacy – the artist in thrall to a landscape or human form who hurries the ephemeral image onto the page or canvas before it disappears and before the artist's self-conscious craft can interfere. Sketches are thus transformed from private and marginalised productions into popular public spectacles, appearing in galleries and ultimately the pages of graphic weeklies such as *Illustrated London News* (est. 1842) with increasing frequency. As Sha notes, between 1769 and 1810, 'the number of sketches versus other works [publicly] shown trebles' (23). But Sha recognises in the form a potential duplicity. The sketch artist evokes authenticity through an artfulness that mimics effortlessness. Two of the painters most commonly associated with the Romantic sketch, J. M. W. Turner (1775–1851) and John Constable (1776–1837), executed their work not with carelessness and immediacy, but with delayed and close attention to detail. For example, Constable's six-foot sketches were not created within the landscapes depicted therein, but 'in the studio' (Sha 1998, 4). Thus, the artist constructs through artificial means the appearance of naturalness and immediacy.

In the following three drawings by William Makepeace Thackeray (1811–63), we can see both forms of sketch – the rough, initial drawing or *schizzo* (Figure 6) and the more refined, self-conscious sketch (Figure 7) – as well as

Figure 6 William Makepeace Thackeray, various sketches (*c.* 1853–4). Robert H. Taylor Collection of English and American Literature (RTC01), no. 145, Manuscripts Division, Department of Rare Books and Special Collections, Princeton University Library. Image courtesy of Princeton University Library. Reproduced with kind permission of Al Murray.

another drawing (Figure 8) that is a sketch only in the broadest sense of the term (the unrefined drawing), and which – through its relationship with the text in which it is housed (*The World*) – is more doodlistic than the other two. Thackeray executed the first two sketches (Figures 6 and 7) while travelling abroad in Continental Europe (1853–4) and writing *The Newcomes* (1855). Appearing together on a single page from an album of Thackeray's works compiled by his granddaughter Hester Ritchie, the drawings demonstrate well the 'rough . . . delineation' described by the *OED* and the rhetorical strategies of naturalness that Sha highlights. The first sketch (Figure 6), numbered 61 in

Figure 7 William Makepeace Thackeray, sketch (*c.* 1853–4). Robert H. Taylor Collection of English and American Literature (RTC01), no. 145, Manuscripts Division, Department of Rare Books and Special Collections, Princeton University Library. Image courtesy of Princeton University Library. Reproduced with kind permission of Al Murray.

the album, embodies what William Gilpin (1792), one of the early theorists of the sketch, describes as 'original sketch[es]', which are best defined as 'plans' rather than 'pictures' (67, 66). Such original sketches are aides-mémoires which allow the sketch artist to record general impressions 'on the spot' (64), but whose '*composition*' (67) and '*expression*' (72) should be refined thereafter (emphases original).[8]

[8] For Gilpin (1792), composition is an idealised representation that – without straying too far – goes beyond the contours of the original sketch or even of the landscape itself, which is 'most defective in composition' and requires assistance (67). He defines *expression* as 'the art of giving each object, that peculiar touch, whether smooth, or rough, which best expresses it's [*sic*] form' (72).

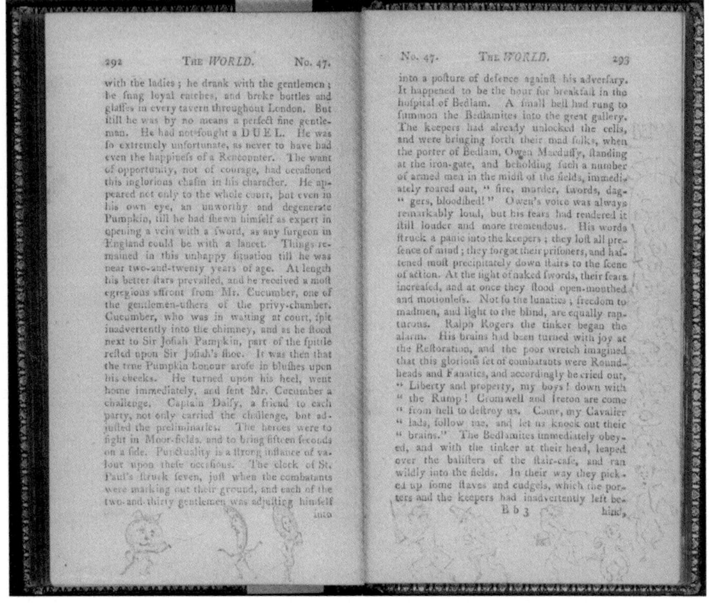

292 THE *WORLD.* No. 47.

with the ladies; he drank with the gentlemen; he ſung loyal catches, and broke bottles and glaſſes in every tavern throughout London. But ſtill he was by no means a perfect fine gentleman. He had not fought a DUEL. He was ſo extremely unfortunate, as never to have had even the happineſs of a Rencounter. The want of opportunity, not of courage, had occaſioned this inglorious chaſm in his character. He appeared not only to the whole court, but even in his own eye, an unworthy and degenerate Pumpkin, till he had ſhewn himſelf as expert in opening a vein with a ſword, as any ſurgeon in England could be with a lancet. Things remained in this unhappy ſituation till he was near two-and-twenty years of age. At length his better ſtars prevailed, and he received a moſt egregious affront from Mr. Cucumber, one of the gentlemen-uſhers of the privy-chamber. Cucumber, who was in waiting at court, ſpit inadvertently into the chimney, and as he ſtood next to Sir Joſiah Pumpkin, part of the ſpittle reſted upon Sir Joſiah's ſhoe. It was then that the true Pumpkin honour aroſe in bluſhes upon his cheeks. He turned upon his heel, went home immediately, and ſent Mr. Cucumber a challenge. Captain Daiſy, a friend to each party, not only carried the challenge, but adjuſted the preliminaries. The heroes were to fight in Moor-fields, and to bring fifteen ſeconds on a ſide. Punctuality is a ſtrong inſtance of valour upon theſe occaſions. The clock of St. Paul's ſtruck ſeven, juſt when the combatants were marking out their ground, and each of the two-and-thirty gentlemen was adjuſting himſelf into

No. 47. THE *WORLD.* 293

into a poſture of defence againſt his adverſary. It happened to be the hour for breakfaſt in the hoſpital of Bedlam. A ſmall bell had rung to ſummon the Bedlamites into the great gallery. The keepers had already unlocked the cells, and were bringing forth their mad folks, when the porter of Bedlam, Owen Macduffy, ſtanding at the iron-gate, and beholding ſuch a number of armed men in the midſt of the fields, immediately roared out, "fire, murder, ſwords, dag-" gers, bloodſhed!" Owen's voice was always remarkably loud, but his fears had rendered it ſtill louder and more tremendous. His words ſtruck a panic into the keepers; they loſt all preſence of mind; they forgot their priſoners, and haſtened moſt precipitately down ſtairs to the ſcene of action. At the ſight of naked ſwords, their fears increaſed, and at once they ſtood open-mouthed and motionleſs. Not ſo the lunatics; freedom to madmen, and light to the blind, are equally rapturous. Ralph Rogers the tinker began the alarm. His brains had been turned with joy at the Reſtoration, and the poor wretch imagined that this glorious ſet of combatants were Roundheads and Fanatics, and accordingly he cried out, "Liberty and property, my boys! down with "the Rump! Cromwell and Ireton are come "from hell to deſtroy us. Come, my Cavalier "lads, follow me, and let us knock out their "brains." The Bedlamites immediately obeyed, and with the tinker at their head, leaped over the baliſters of the ſtair-caſe, and ran wildly into the fields. In their way they picked up ſome ſtaves and cudgels, which the porters and the keepers had inadvertently left be-

Bb 3 hind,

Figure 8 William Makepeace Thackeray, marginal drawings (n.d.). From *The World*, vol. 1 (1795), ed. by Edward Moore, pages 292–93. Haverford College Libraries, Quaker and Special Collections, Rare Books PR1365. W56 1795. Image courtesy of Haverford College Libraries, Quaker and Special Collections. Reproduced with kind permission of Al Murray.

Like Figure 6, Figure 7 represents Thackeray's effort to capture a landscape(s), although it is a much more polished and detailed attempt. Depicting a street view from his trip, this roadside sketch imbues the town with quaint, picturesque charm. Gilpin (1792) argues that the purpose of the sketch as a category of expression is to produce this 'picturesque beauty' (the subject of the first essay in *Three Essays*), which he defines as beauty mediated in graphic form and distinguishes from simple beauty, which resides in objects themselves and is perceivable directly through the senses. According to Gilpin, drawing that is too 'neat and smooth' paralyses the inherent beauty and dynamism of real objects – despite the latter's own smoothness and elegance (4). Such a drawing fails to capture, for example, the play of light on a building's surface or the movement of trees in the wind. The sketch seeks to overcome those limitations by creating dynamic effects through 'contrast' (20), 'action' (12), 'decisive[ness]' (17), 'variety' (20), and 'richness' (20) of light and colour. That is, artists use a carefully contrived roughness (or, more precisely, ruggedness) to imbue their pictures with naturalness and liveliness that belie their artifice.[9]

Unlike these two sketches, Thackeray's third set of drawings (Figure 8) are sketches in only the broadest understanding of the term. They are quick and unrefined drawings – 'sprightly pencil designs', as a Henry Sotheran Ltd (1879) sales catalogue describes them (4) – that illustrate Thackeray's personal copy of the four-volume 1795 reprint of *The World*, edited by Edward Moore (1712–57). Currently owned by Haverford College in Pennsylvania, these volumes contain a number of similar 'sketches', as the library catalogue describes them, but the use of the term *sketch* speaks primarily to their graphic method or material (loose strokes, pencil, etc.) and not their substance or genre.

Thackeray's comical drawings in Figure 8, from the first volume of the set, illustrate letter no. 47 by Mary Muzzy, pseudonym of John Boyle, Earl of Cork and Orrery (1707–62), which recounts the satirical story of Mary's grandfather, Sir Josiah Pumpkin, and his duel with Mr Cucumber. The duel, adjudicated by Captain Daisy and with fifteen 'seconds' on each side, devolves into a rout by the escaped inhabitants of nearby Bedlam Hospital. While one might see some similarities in the way that Thackeray rendered the figures in Figures 6 and 8, the latter set of drawings takes place within a different context, namely Thackeray's engagement with Boyle's letter. The drawings are closer to readers' marks in this regard; they are evidence of

[9] Gilpin (1792) differentiates between roughness, which 'relates only to the surface of bodies', and ruggedness, the term appropriate to use 'when we speak of their delineation' (6–7).

use, reading, and, to some extent, interpretation. But these marks are not the manicules and glosses that demonstrate close reading. They illustrate the text in the sense that they present a graphic representation of action and characters within the letter – although Thackeray takes some comic liberties in his renderings of Sir Pumpkin, Mr Cucumber, and Captain Daisy. No evidence suggests, however, that Thackeray planned to publish an illustrated edition of *The World*; insofar as we can tell, he did not intend the drawings to serve as preparatory work for a more refined picture or illustration. Thackeray decorated far too many of his books for the presence of these drawings alone to suggest that he had any special plan for an illustrated version of *The World*. Instead, he was playing in the margins for his own amusement, engaging digressively in dramatising the text. While largely reinforcing rather than destabilising the meaning of the text, the drawings nonetheless bring the work into focus as Thackeray saw it and remind us of Roland Barthes's (1977) maxim that a 'text's unity lies not in its origin but in its destination' (148).

More than a trace of his reading, Thackeray's copy of *The World* inscribes a new pictorial and doubly comic version of the text within its pages. The book provides evidence of the degree to which Thackeray was steeped in the comic tradition of English literature and more generally connects textual genesis and reception by revealing the ways in which Thackeray's reading translated so easily into the composition of new works. In describing Thackeray's habit of doodling, Joseph Grego (1879) noted Thackeray's 'facility for making rapid little pictures on the inspiration of the moment', and one sees that habit at work in this set of drawings (xiii). That is, one sees not illustration or adaptation but a spontaneous delighting in the pleasures of the moment – the 'bright, ready *croquis* of the instant' as opposed to the 'oppressive' and 'laboured' work of serious art (xiii). Although a sketch in the sense that it is figurative and unpolished, Thackeray's drawing shares with that form neither its purpose to record a momentary impression for posterity nor its destiny to become a more refined drawing. The drawing instead embodies play and recursive signification, an over- and reinscribing of meaning that is directed towards only the doodler and any chance viewers of his personal copy of the book. As such it becomes a doodle rather than the kinds of sketches represented in Figures 6 and 7.

3 Cartoons and Caricatures

Thackeray's comic figures (Figure 8) and Wilde's profile sketches (Figure 1) remind us that doodles often take the form of simple, silly, or exaggerated faces. David Maclagan (2014) has made the same point, noting that doodles 'often have a strong human presence, in the form of faces, figures, and actions' (66). He sees these figures and faces, alongside more abstract motifs and ornamental designs, as forming a 'subliminal kind of pictorial lingua franca' (21). But doodlers are not consciously working with an established visual vocabulary. How, then, are they conditioned to draw from this graphic lexicon? And how do doodles relate to the other genres of comic drawing that share the vocabulary of exaggerated, funny, or grotesque figuration?

The period preceding the point at which doodle acquires its modern meaning (i.e., the long nineteenth century) is marked by an increasingly democratising literary culture consisting of richly illustrated and mass-produced periodical and monographic publications. The growth of this progressively pictorial mass media shapes the visual imagination of doodlers throughout the nineteenth century and beyond. Occupying a central place in that shifting print culture was the magazine to which Thackeray was a regular contributor, *Punch, or The London Charivari* (est. 1841). Densely illustrated, *Punch* employed its stable of artists to produce a range of comic engravings for the magazine and in so doing gave new meaning to the terms *cartoon*, *comic*, and *caricature*. The first of these terms derives from *cartone* ('large sheet of drawing-paper'): the full-scale, 'fully rendered illustrations' that Renaissance artists often used to 'transfer the drawing to the surface that would contain the finished work' (Fennell 1892, 210; Culotta 2021, n.p.).[10] The cartoon in its original usage was thus a penultimate step before the execution of the fully realised painting, tapestry, or fresco but after the *primi pensieri* and other early sketches that we discussed earlier. *Punch* gave the term new meaning in 1843. After the medieval Palace of Westminster burned down in 1834, the government established the Fine Art Commission to oversee the interior design of the

[10] See also Harvey 2009, 26; and, for a detailed history of Renaissance *cartoni*, Bambach 1999.

building's successor. The Commission sponsored a design competition for large-scale cartoons of historical subjects. John Leech (1817–64) satirised the competitive exhibition as out of touch with the needs of the poor in *Cartoon, No 1: Substance and Shadow* (July 1843), the first in a series of 'Mr. Punch's cartoons', which inaugurated the modern usage of 'cartoon' to refer to 'a combination of words and pictures that can tell a story, share a thought, articulate an emotion, promote a point of view, or make people laugh' (Walker 2022, 24). The term came to be applied to 'all of the drawings' in *Punch*, becoming a genre of magazine illustration that extended far beyond its original source.[11]

The satirical, puckish nature of Leech's original cartoon and all of *Punch*'s drawings lent the term a sense of play and critique. The magazine had already drawn on a tradition of caricature partly embodied by the political magazines founded in France by Charles Philipon (1806–62): *La Caricature* (est. 1830) and a second, more literary magazine, *Le Charivari* (est. 1832), from which *Punch* borrowed its subtitle, 'The English Charivari' (Harvey 2009, 26). The history of caricature is as old as literature and art (Wright 1875), but the modern understanding of the genre develops in parallel to the eighteenth- and nineteenth-century trends in periodical publishing that we have been tracing. In this context, caricature largely takes the form of grotesque representations of individuals for satirical or humorous effect. As David Carrier (2000) explains, caricature is 'inherently an art of exaggeration', which involves 'deformation' (16). Or in the words of caricaturist par excellence Max Beerbohm (1872–1954), caricature is 'the art of exaggerating, without fear or favour, the peculiarities of this or that human body, for the mere sake of exaggeration' (Beerbohm 1928, 210). Figure 9 is a typical example of the form in which *Punch* turns navy admiral Sir Charles Napier (1786–1860) into a pictorial capital that renders him comical, elongating his nose to mimic the appearance of a ship and underscore his superciliousness. One can see this same principle at play in any number of examples. For instance, Beerbohm clearly applies this principle of exaggeration to a rendering of G. K. Chesterton (1874–1936) in the 11 June 1904 issue of

[11] As the *OED* defines it, cartoon came to represent 'full-page illustration[s] in a paper or periodical' and, thereafter, 'humorous or topical drawing[s] (of any size) in a newspaper' or related publication.

PUNCH, OR THE LON[

PUNCH'S MIRROR OF PARLIAMENT.

[F]IRST DEBATE ON THE NAVY.—SIR C. NAPIER, in moving for a Select Committee on the Construction of Ships, was anxious to put upon the navy the best construction possible. He (SIR C. NAPIER) in looking at the 50-gun ships, and taking them critically to pieces, thought that taking them literally to pieces was the best thing that could be done with them. (*Hear, and a laugh.*) An experiment had been made by cutting down bad vessels into good, but you might as well cut down a worn-out Wellington into an effective highlow. (*Loud cheers.*) As to the 18-gun vessels, they had gone through as many transformations as a trick in a pantomime. Then there was the *Vanguard*, which had plenty of guns, but if she used them she would set herself on fire. Then there was the *Queen*, which his hon. friend MR. C. WOOD was so much in love with, that he ordered six more *Queens*, which would be in fact restoring the Heptarchy. The *Queen* rolled easily, pitched easily, was strong-built, but had never been seen scudding under a very heavy sea. He now came to steam-boats. There was the *Gorgon* war-frigate, which was very well adapted for running away but not for fighting, because it only had one available gun, and that was more likely to hit the officer in command than any other person. (*A laugh.*) He concluded by moving for a Select Committee to know what money had been voted for building ships, and what the dickens had been done with it.

Figure 9 Caricature/pictorial capital, 'Punch's Mirror of Parliament', *Punch* 8, no. 189 (22 February 1845), page 89 (Ledger author: Gilbert Abbott à Beckett). Public domain. Image from copy held at University of California Libraries, available at hathitrust.org.

Harpers Weekly.[12] Homing in on Chesterton's weight, Beerbohm not only underscores a distinctive physical feature, but he also extracts something of Chesterton's gregariousness and outsized presence by doing so.

[12] See Max Beerbohm, 'G. K. Chesterton as Seen by Max Beerbohm', *Harper's Weekly* 48, part 1 (11 June 1904), p. 901. https://hdl.handle.net/2027/mdp.39015030326501?urlappend=%3Bseq=864%3Bownerid=113958092-863.

Like doodles, caricatures inhabit a space between art and literature, a point reinforced by the pictogrammatic nature of *Punch*'s drawing. Critics and scholars have traditionally held caricature's visual qualities in 'low or at best modest estimation', seeing them as a form of 'ephemeral popular culture and political propaganda' (Haywood 2013, 7). While these two examples are accomplished drawings, we can also see that refinement and execution are somewhat beside the point. In fact, Rodolphe Töpffer ((1845) 1965) emphatically argues in *Essay on Physiognomy* that comical drawings are preferably executed maladroitly:

> Especially for humorous or whimsical subjects, a clumsy daring that jumps somewhat rudely, with all fours, on the end in view (at the risk of missing a few details and smashing a few forms) has usually hit the mark better than a talent more practiced but more timid, which ambles slowly down all the meanders of elegant execution and careful imitation. (8–9)

E. H. Gombrich and Ernst Kris (1940) amplify this point, arguing that a high quality of draughtsmanship can be counterproductive for caricature: 'in so far as caricature is a graphic joke, it no more requires a painter's gift than a skilled punner must be a poet' (18). Witty but untalented draughtsmen 'were often funnier', in Gombrich and Kris's opinion, than their skilled counterparts because they produced both 'intentional and unintentional humour', which 'professional artist[s] soon learnt to adopt' (18). Caricaturists thus deploy a strategic crudeness that makes their designs visually similar to sketches and doodles, even though the former are directed towards political ends while the latter are generally apolitical.

G. K. Chesterton's best-known notebook ('The Notebook') contains a prodigious number of amusing figures and faces – including many apparent caricatures – interspersed among the draft poems and other literary fragments. Drawings of William Gladstone (1809–98) and T. H. Huxley (1825–95), such as those in Figure 10, are especially prominent. Upon first glance, one can see Chesterton's skill as a comic illustrator, particularly in the more fully refined drawing of Gladstone. The renderings of Huxley appear more gestational, perhaps evidence of Chesterton's experiments with form, line,

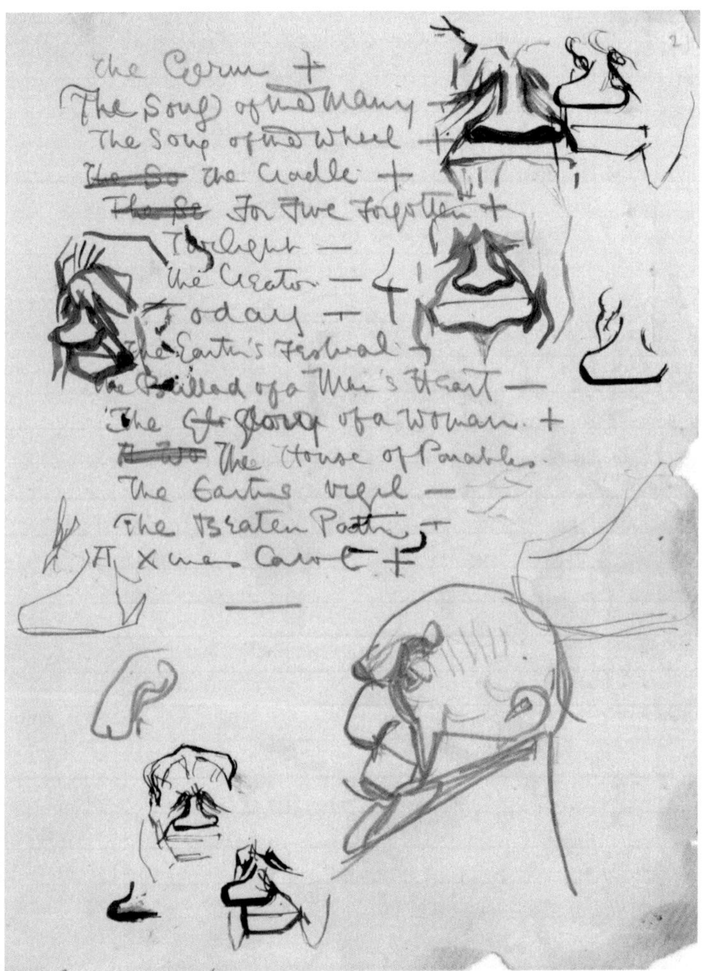

Figure 10 G. K. Chesterton, doodles of William Gladstone and Thomas Huxley, untitled holograph notebook (1894–6). British Library, Add MS 73334, MS page 2 recto. Image courtesy of the British Library. Reproduced by permission of United Agents Ltd on behalf of the Royal Literary Fund.

and perspective, his working through sketching towards a more fully realised version of Huxley. The drawings of both figures possess some attributes of early sketches and seem clearly to be caricatures. The exaggerated features of each render them both comical: Huxley's hangdog appearance and Gladstone's excessive solemnity. While indeed they are caricatures in both appearance and function – Chesterton is at least partly satirising the debate between Huxley and Gladstone concerning the Gadarene swine (see Chesterton (1935) 2012, 28) – their status as both sketches and caricatures is undercut or at least minimised when placed in the context of the entire notebook, which includes drawings of Gladstone and/or Huxley on at least 50 of the notebook's 170 pages. What at first seem to be deliberate caricatures (preliminary or otherwise) start to assume the form of doodles upon closer inspection. Chesterton's drawings become not so much satires but visual habits. They are stereotypic interruptions and vandalisations of the literary manuscript, despite the fact that the desecrated text is Chesterton's. The proliferation of the caricatures shifts their subjects from Huxley and Gladstone to Chesterton's own mind and habits. Engaging with these drawings, one is prompted to wonder less about their subjects and more about Chesterton's obsession with them (or at least their forms) and the role that this general graphomania plays within his practice as a writer and thinker.

Through repetition, these two figures become anchors of a visual vocabulary for Chesterton that is conditioned by the widespread presence in British culture of political cartoons and Gladstone's and Huxley's prominence within them. Gladstone's likeness, for example, proliferated in the illustrated press and adorned numerous commercial goods; among these many representations, the Gladstone cartoons alone, Asa Briggs (1998) estimates, were 'legion', including numerous examples from *Punch* (49). More important, the role that these drawings play in the notebook, primarily a literary manuscript like Wilde's, transforms our understanding of the text therein. The Gladstone and Huxley doodles en masse are not caricatures of either man, although individually they appear to be. Instead, the images together serve as a framework or leitmotif, a mostly subliminal impulse encapsulating the tension between pessimistic agnosticism and exuberant faith that animates the literary content of the notebook as well as Chesterton's personal, self-professed doctrinal questing during his time as a student at the Slade School of Art. Chesterton's drawings of

Gladstone and Huxley are comical representations whose ostensible purpose is effaced but whose childlike jouissance and repetition, despite the drawings' digressiveness, suffuse the text with added meaning. The sketches present individually as caricatures and cartoons but are revealed as doodles when one juxtaposes them with the text or analyses them collectively.

As a 'graphic expression of Wit', in Gombrich and Kris's (1940) words, caricatures disrupt 'well-established meaning'; they temporarily 'cast off the bridles which restrain our aggressive impulses and prescribe the strict path of logic to our thought' (26–27). Whereas caricature is a negation or subversion of meaning, doodles facilitate a double negation and further destabilise even the language of graphic wit. Caricatures are dialogic; they speak to and about their audiences. Doodles are instead the somewhat unintentional, but not unadulterated language that borrows a recognisable vocabulary of symbol and design but invests it with new, sometimes inscrutable or excessive meaning.

4 Illustrations and Grangerisations

As page-mates to literary texts, doodles can mimic yet another genre of graphic work: the illustration. Like other genres considered herein, textual illustration has a long history extending back to the beginning of human culture. But nineteenth-century developments in literary culture and technology gave rise to new forms of illustration that coalesced into a formal genre and fed into the habits and visual lexicons of literary authors and readers. Inventions such as xylography and steam-powered printing not only increased the number of illustrated texts available to readers, but they also reoriented the relationship of word and image on the same mass-produced pages (Lauster 2007, 35).[13] One can see the intermingling of word and image – in fact, the primacy of the image as it cuts across the verbal text – and a concomitant demarginalisation of pictorial content that these processes fostered on this page (Figure 11) from volume six (1844) of *Punch*, which was itself co-founded by Ebenezer Landells (1808–60), student of xylography's pioneer, Thomas Bewick (1753–1828).[14] The increasing ease, fidelity, and professionalism with which pictorial content could be reproduced created a self-perpetuating condition in which readers not only became acclimated to but also expected the presence of graphic content in books and serials. By century's close, the demand had 'become so great that few books were published without some pictorial content' (Kooistra 1995, 1).

The nineteenth-century boom in illustrated publishing drew on a pluripotent stew of pictorial content that would later settle into distinct graphic genres: sketches, cartoons, comics, and caricatures (among others). In the early part of the century, the term *illustration* largely denoted any of the various genres of line drawing regularly featured in publications like the *Illustrated London News* (est. 1842), the *Illuminated Magazine* (1843–5), and the *Illustrated Times* (1855–72), whose titles signalled to their readers the presence of pictorial content in general more than any specific generic or

[13] William Blake's invention of relief etching around 1788 represents an alternate method of printing word and image in close integration; however, few other artists employed this same technique.

[14] Although Landells had left the magazine by the end of 1842. (See Doran 2004.)

A happy New Year, my Masters!

IT shall be no fault of PUNCH, if there is in all the land one honest kindly heart, that is not blythe from this—the Young Year's birthday—till the funeral knell of Old December. You see the banquet our fancy has prepared for you—for thus should you fare and revel were our garret as large as our love; but we are "cabin'd, cribb'd, confin'd;" and, potent as we are, we cannot crowd our myriad of friends into a nutshell. Pshaw!—There is not a morsel so tooth-some but it palls upon the palate—no draught so sweet or potent but it brings satiety. We will make you merrier and wiser than you could grow on rare meats and strong wines. Our Table of Contents shall teem with *piquant* jests and *pungent* satires; dainty pieces of wisdom garnished with motley carvings; draughts deep and sparkling, drawn from Hippocrene itself; whilst our "Roo-too-tooit" shall sound like the dulcet tones of Apollo's shell, harmonised, as it will be, with your own heartstrings.

The months shall circle round you to such joyous measures, that you will scarcely miss the flowers of Spring, or feel the iciness of Winter.—— Come! pass another year with

PUNCH.

NEW YEAR'S DAY, 1844.

No. 130.

Figure 11 'A Happy New Year, My Masters', *Punch* 6 (January/June 1844). Public domain. Image from copy held at the Library of Congress, available at www.loc.gov/resource/gdclccn.10003698v06.

interpretive approach. As the century progressed, illustration began to concretise into a distinct genre that would become familiar through the well-known illustrated fiction of authors such as Dickens, Thackeray, and Lewis Carroll. This genre itself evolved in parallel with other commercial, industrial, literary, and artistic trends. The comic sketches of 'relatively untutored' illustrators of the 1830s and 1840s, such as Cruikshank and Doyle (Goldman and Cooke 2012, 1), ceded ground later in the century to a professional class of formally trained artists who worked in a 'socially realistic style' (Allingham 2012, 178). Still later in the century, as Aestheticism shaded into Decadence, illustrators such as Aubrey Beardsley adopted a less naturalistic, more fantastical and antagonistic style that inaugurated a 'third period of the illustrated book' (Golden 2017, 3). These stylistic shifts throughout the century, although by no means simply linear, informed the visual lexicon from which doodlers took their forms and figures.

In its broadest sense – that is, in the sense etymologically derived from '*illustrāre*' ('to light up, illuminate, clear up, elucidate, embellish') – illustration is a genre whose aim is to 'elucidate . . . by means of drawings or pictures', or 'to ornament (a book, etc.) in this way with elucidatory designs' ('Illustrate', *OED online*). As Paul Goldman (2012) argues, such a definition implies that illustration is 'but a short step from interpretation' (15). Philip James (1947) draws this connection more explicitly, describing illustration as 'a partnership between author and artist to which the artist contributes something which is a pictorial comment on the author's words or an interpretation of his meaning in another medium' (7). Although illustrations elucidate or comment on texts, they do so in varied ways. Lorraine Janzen Kooistra (1995) has identified a spectrum of word–image relationships that define illustration, ranging from relatively straightforward representations of the text, which she calls strategies of *quotation*, to more desultory strategies such as those that she terms *impression* and *parody*.

On one end of the spectrum, quotational illustrations – although they never correspond exactly to the verbal text – more or less faithfully represent their corresponding verbal texts.[15] For example, 'Phiz' (Hablot

[15] Kooistra (1995) defines 'quotation' as the method of illustration in which the 'artist produces a picture which is a visual double for the word in much the same way that

Knight Browne, 1815–82) employs this strategy in his 'Paul and Mrs. Pipchin' (Figure 12) for Charles Dickens's *Dombey and Son* (1848). In the novel's corresponding passage, Dickens describes the scene with the younger Paul Dombey and his boarding-house matron: 'At this exemplary old lady, Paul would sit staring in his little armchair by the fire.'[16] Phiz's drawing recreates Dickens's language. And even Mrs. Pipchin's grotesque, Punchinella appearance – one that easily conjures Browne's comic work for *Punch* – credibly renders Dickens's description of her appearance as an 'ogress and child-queller', with a 'mottled face' and a 'hook nose' ((1848) 1974, 100). On the other end of the spectrum, impressionistic and parodic illustrations happily engage in idiosyncratic or antagonistic ways with their source texts. Kooistra (1995) defines 'impression', quoting Oscar Wilde's 'The Critic as Artist', as a digressive illustrational approach in which 'the artist . . . deals with the verbal text "simply as a starting point for a new creation"' (17), whereas a parodic illustration centres the source text but 'disrupts the authority of the word', targeting the 'gaps, indeterminacies and contradictions in the verbal text' (19). Charles Ricketts (1866–1931) combines elements of both strategies in his unpublished illustration for Wilde's prose poem 'The Artist'.[17] Recreating aspects of Wilde's story about Narcissus, Ricketts nonetheless adds extraneous, non-diagetic elements that he borrows from another of Wilde's prose poems, 'The Poet'; namely he adds the figure of the centaur, a visual representation of

literary critics copy a section of the work under investigation into their own texts' (15), but she warns that the '*quotation* strategy in image/text relations can never simply be a referential/deferential arrangement whereby the visual simply copies or translates the verbal in pictorial form' (16). The act of duplication – however straightforward – creates both an amplificatory and 'meta-critical' difference (16).

16 Not only does the drawing accurately capture the story's action and characters, but Dickens also dictated the image's composition directly. Writing in a letter to his biographer John Forster (4 November 1846), Dickens suggested that the 'best subject for Browne will be at Mrs. Pipchin's; and if he liked to do a quiet odd thing, Paul, Mrs. Pipchin, and the Cat, by the fire' (Dickens 1977, 653).

17 For a reproduction and extended close reading, see Mercurio 2011, 10, fig. 1.

Figure 12 'Phiz' (Hablot Knight Browne), 'Paul and Mrs. Pipchin'. In *Dombey and Son*, by Charles Dickens. London: Bradbury and Evans, 1848. Public domain. Image from copy held at University of California Libraries, available at hathitrust.org.

both orality and debauchery.[18] The centaur allows Ricketts to digress from 'The Artist', to challenge Wilde's own notion that storytelling is more dynamic than visual art, and to rebuke (albeit mildly) Wilde's personal excesses.

Whether faithful, antagonistic, or digressive, illustration accompanies and concerns itself – at least initially – with the written or printed text. Doodles are often similarly situated in the same paginal space as a literary text, but their relationships to those texts are very different from the ones that Kooistra describes. First, doodlers do not necessarily employ conscious or deliberate strategies of commenting when they doodle on a text, although the effects of doodling can sometimes be similarly echoic, oblique, or parodic. The verbal text is itself not necessarily primary; doodles' composition can and often does antedate the composition of the linguistic text. Furthermore, doodling is not complicit in the formal publishing apparatus that defines illustration – in fact, it is often antithetical to the aims and mechanisms of professional publishing. Doodles exist in drafts, scraps of papers, and post-print grangerisations; they are not, unless clandestinely, part of the formal design process that leads to the production of illustrated texts. Like the sketch, the illustration is shadowed by its final form and carries with it the knowledge of its audiences: the authors, printers, engravers, readers, and so on whose expectations and habits shape the illustrator's design; the doodle, conversely, is often an end unto itself.

Compelling evidence that doodling and illustration are separate genres comes from the example of Max Beerbohm (1953), who expressed a strong antipathy towards illustrated fiction:

> I do not like to read a novel in an illustrated edition. . . . If I cannot see the characters in a novel, then they are not worth seeing. If I can see them, then any other man's definite presentment of them seems to be an act of impertinence to myself and of impiety to the author. (65)

[18] Ricketts associates the action of Wilde's storytelling with the motion of the centaur in 'The Poet' (Ricketts (1932) 2011, 17).

Whether Beerbohm intended this statement as a critique of realistic illustration or of all illustrated texts, he nonetheless (typically) adhered to this principle in his own published literary works, which were largely free of pictorial content. But Beerbohm's distaste for illustrated editions was no barrier to his doodling in both the early manuscript draft and first print edition of his only novel, *Zuleika Dobson* (started 1898; published by Heinemann in 1911).

Like many of Beerbohm's rough drafts, the early manuscript of *Zuleika Dobson* (representing chapters 9–13 and 15–24 of the published novel) contains numerous pencilled doodles and other visual embellishments – more than one hundred by the count of N. John Hall (1985, n.p.). Beerbohm omitted these doodles from subsequent drafts as he worked towards publication, as one can see in a second, embellishment-free draft of the novel that is also held at Princeton University. Beerbohm's act of expungement reinforces his anti-illustration credo. The drawings from the early manuscript are not illustrations, despite the fact that the manuscript is closer in form to another kind of illustration that Kooistra (1995) calls 'cross-dressing', in which a single author/artist composes the illustrated book and thereby collapses the 'traditional distinctions between writing and drawing' (206). Beerbohm neither executed the drawings for an illustrated edition of the novel, nor did he intend them for an audience of anyone other than himself. His primary purpose in creating them, in his words, was to 'refresh the fatigued scribe' (quoted in Viscusi 1979, 235). The drawings are thus escapes from the tedium and strain of literary composition; however, they are also an essential aspect of Beerbohm's writing. Without these 'random scribbles', as he called them, Beerbohm's attention, imagination, and stamina might have flagged (quoted in Viscusi 1979, 235). More important, the doodles are not simply brief and unrelated reprieves from the labour of writing. The drawings – many of which represent the novel's characters – are also moments of play that invoke, inform, demarcate, reframe, and disassemble (but rarely elucidate) the verbal text.

The early *Zuleika* draft is part of the series of documents that form the novel's history. Jean Bellemin-Noël first called such textual artefacts the *avant-texte* (pre-text): the 'sketches, manuscripts, proofs, and "variants" – all of the material which precedes a work and which can form a single textual system with that work' (quoted in and translated by Davis 2002, 92). *Critique génétique*, or 'genetic criticism', is the study of these pre-texts and, by extension, literary origins. Laurent Jenny (1996) finds in the study of these pre-texts, though, a paradox: the finished literary work is the motivation for genetic criticism but not its object of study. Genetic criticism either offers commentary on a finished work, reinscribing that work with its pre-textual history, or it is the study of writing itself. In both cases, the pre-text is a destabilising force: the critical effort is directed towards either the construction of an unachievable corpus, which must include all extant pre-texts – transmuted through analysis and editing into texts themselves – and the finished work, or the representation of writing and its concomitant mentation. In the case of the latter, as Jenny argues, 'the traces of "writing" are necessarily incomplete in relation to the process of mental creation . . . to which they refer and of which they are the irregular evidence' (15). Jenny argues that the work of genetic criticism is both impractical and impossible, but implicit in this charge is a sense – derived from the term itself – that the goal of genetic theory is interpretation (i.e., criticism). But the tools of genetic criticism – or at least its objects of study, including doodles – could be deployed towards a different, post-critical enterprise. Although sceptical of genetic methodologies, Jenny himself notes the possibility of non-interpretive goals, describing the study of pre-texts as the point of affective return to the moment of scribal thought, to 'the real of a creation starting with the written traces' (22). He illustrates this effort to 'redynamize the trace so as to relive the event' of writing by citing Pierre-Marc de Biasi's description of reading Flaubert's notebooks:

> The handwriting, jerky, often difficult to decipher, sometimes 'seismographic' is clearly characteristic of the uncomfortable positions in which the author took his notes, naturally with a pencil. In certain places one can unmistakably recognize the shaking of the carriage going over the cobblestones. (Quoted in Jenny 1996, 22)

One can retrace a similar yet more comfortable authorial experience in Beerbohm's early *Zuleika* manuscript. On MS p. 12 (Figure 13), one can see not only emendations and cancellations that mark the literary manuscript as a work in process – a work that, in Beerbohm's words, 'shows the sentences

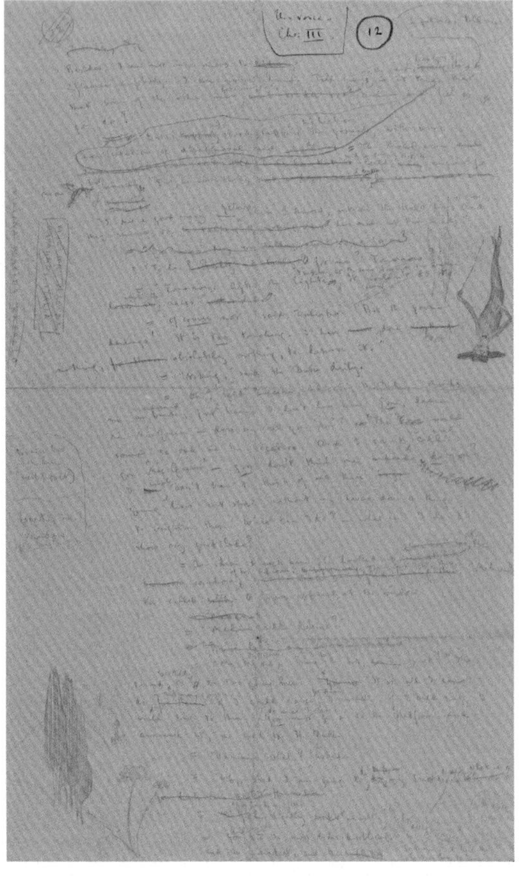

Figure 13 Max Beerbohm, holograph manuscript of *Zuleika Dobson* with doodles. Princeton University Library, Department of Rare Books and Special Collections, Manuscripts Division, Robert H. Taylor Collection of English and American Literature, RTC01, no. 187, MS page 12 recto. Image courtesy of Princeton University Library. Reproduced with permission of Berlin Associates.

in the act of growing, and of being pruned and tended' (quoted in Viscusi 1979, 235) – but also signs of Beerbohm's experience of living and writing at the time. The page contains various forms of play and interpolation: two pencil drawings and the written address 'Villina Placida, Rapallo, Italia'. Unlike illustrations, the two drawings are unrelated to the verbal text; however, they do reconstruct the scene of the novel's creation. In one drawing is Beerbohm himself, walking in the Ligurian Apennines near his home, or, as Robert Viscusi (1979) describes him, 'in his new guise of *gentiluomo inglese* . . . among the Lombardy poplars' (250). The repeated name of his home also evokes Beerbohm's state of mind: he rechristens (and re-genders) his house, Villino Chiaro, as Villina Placida. Both the drawings and invocation of his residence suggest that Beerbohm is at peace in his Italian surroundings, afforded the mental and physical space to concentrate on his writing. In this sense, the doodles (verbal and visual) seem to function, as Beerbohm explained, to 'refresh' himself; they are distractions from the writing, ones that re-anchor and resituate him in his physical location from which he draws strength. Readers of this pre-text can thus locate Beerbohm within his surroundings and make inferences about his state of mind, even if one cannot peer with a magnifying glass into the author's brain as Zuleika does to another character, E. J. Craddock, in a different set of drawings from Beerbohm's manuscript.[19]

The ways in which Flaubert's notebooks or Beerbohm's doodles situate the reader in a pre-/post-critical space runs counter to what Rita Felski (2015) has called a 'hypercritical style of analysis that has crowded out alternative forms of

[19] For a reproduction of this drawing, see illustration 15 from Mercurio and Gabelman 2019, 32. Beerbohm's drawing alludes to a scene in the novel in which Beerbohm as narrator revisits his old room in Merton College, now occupied by Craddock. Beerbohm eschews 'peer[ing] over his shoulder at [the] MS' of Craddock's will, in which Craddock leaves all his possessions to Zuleika. Beerbohm (1911) instead directly reads Craddock's mind – 'the writer's brain was open to me' (188). Beerbohm's doodle of Zuleika is not a (re)presentation or even interpretation of the text but a conflation of Zuleika and Beerbohm (who is already identified with Craddock by dint of the latter's occupation of Beerbohm's old room), underscoring the self-referential and self-contained nature of Beerbohm's text.

intellectual life' (10). Jenny (1996) questions the aims of genetic criticism precisely because it sidesteps normal modes of critique, valuing opacity over clarity and studying the 'very instability' of the pre-text, 'where explicit projects, unconscious choices, and the play between what is possible and what is dangerous are intertwined to the point of nonsense' (10). Despite Jenny's reservations, the scholarly return to the point of literary origin is revealing and valid if one's aim is not the elucidation of the finished text or the full state of the author's mind but – acknowledging the inchoateness of literary genesis – the understanding and experience, however impartial or imprecise, of the processes of literary creation both individual and general. Literature derives from a practice of ideating, researching, writing, reconceptualising, and rewriting, and even the published work is not necessarily the terminus of that process. The case of Coleridge's 'at least eighteen' revisions of *The Rime of the Ancient Mariner* is a well-known, if extreme example of this point. (See Stillinger 1994, 60.) Moreover, the act of writing is both conscious and visceral. To return to a text's genesis is to return to an artefact of the author's experience of writing, inclusive of its conscious and subconscious elements. With its aim of elucidation, illustration is aligned with critique (and against doodling) in its search for textual meaning. Doodles challenge such modes of interpretation, further underscoring the generic differences between the two art forms.

Doodling represents a form of non- or counter-signification. In the context of literary manuscripts, doodles also threaten traditional boundaries between writing and drawing. Authors' early manuscripts are the scene of latent thought and tumultuous effort and, like writers' notebooks, they possess chaotic, sometimes indecipherable potentiality. In the primordial soup of the early literary manuscript, word and image are closer to their shared and embryonic state of being: the line. As Jean-Luc Nancy (2013) has argued, '[d]rawing is the opening of form', by which he means both opening – in the sense of 'beginning, departure, origin, dispatch, impetus, or sketching out' – and 'availability or inherent capacity' (1). As authors begin to call their literary works into being, they gesture towards both demarcation and fulfilment. Doodles might thus embody pluripotency, but they also often function as *pharmaka* in the Derridean sense, as both 'remedy and poison' (Derrida 1981, 70); doodling can aid writing, but just as frequently it can trouble it. Whereas even the most antagonistic illustrations function dialectically in relationship to their source text, doodles demarcate a contested space of 'legible' and 'illegible' writing (Reid 1994, 6). Unlike the 'established signs' of legible writing, '[i]llegible writing shows things to be what they are not'; it 'indicates . . . that the sign has been remorsefully eaten away by its own figurative nature, and that it does indeed take almost nothing at all for the figure to resort back to its status as a mere drawing' (6). Martine Reid elaborates on this point as it pertains to the literary draft:

> As it follows the train of thought to which it gives body and movement, the writing process comes across as a work-form that is forever on the point of drifting off course. And it is there in the hazardous limbo between the legible and the visible that the illusory barrier between one domain and another is erased. And graphic representation appears: it appears during the pauses and hesitations of the thought process, when the pen can be caught accomplishing other gestures: additions, scribbles, and the excessive embellishment of letters, the transformation of words, lines, and inkblots into heads, animals (reviving some 'mimological' effect), or other, less creditable things – 'the hand talks', says [Jean] Dubuffet. The visible returns and jostles with the legible: it is unpretentious, playful, useless, and it draws writing towards mocking, childish counterwriting. (7)

To study literary manuscripts is thus to investigate the ways in which literature arises from a contest between sense and nonsense, symbol and line. These drafts and their doodles remind us of this dialectic at play in those spaces, a dialectic that is both evident through the doodles, emendations, and cancellations of literary drafts and just beneath the surface of the published text.

The conflation of word and image also collapses the temporally linear relationship between word and image that defines traditional modes of illustration in which textual composition precedes pictorial illumination. For example, Figure 14 shows the ways in which Beerbohm's writing derives from his drawing. Although skilled in both arts, Beerbohm's

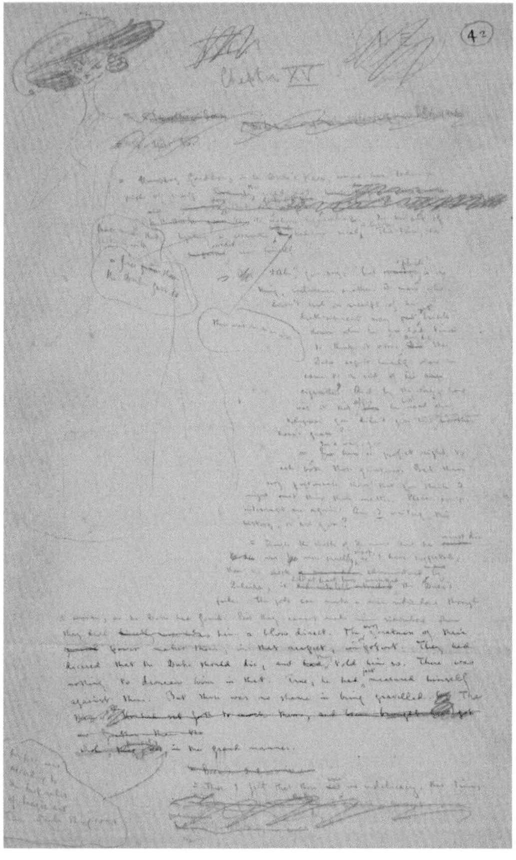

42

Chapter XV

Figure 14 Max Beerbohm, holograph manuscript of *Zuleika Dobson* with doodle. Princeton University Library, Department of Rare Books and Special Collections, Manuscripts Division, Robert H. Taylor Collection of English and American Literature, RTC01, no. 187, MS page 42 recto. Image courtesy of Princeton University Library. Reproduced with permission of Berlin Associates.

drawings, according to Robert Viscusi (1979), 'came more easily to him than words and were always the surest conduit to his imagination' (249). Beerbohm 'destroyed' the drafts of the novel's first chapters, making it difficult to know what role the drawings played in *Zuleika*'s earliest formulations. Nonetheless, we can see in Figure 14 the primacy of Zuleika's image within the manuscript page. The drawing of Zuleika occupies more than half the page height, and her dress extends horizontally to the midway point of the page. One sees the words bend around the dress, signifying that their composition – at least on this page – post-dates that of the drawing's. The graphic image of Zuleika dominates this page and Beerbohm's many visual sketches of his character are plausibly the source of the novel's verbal descriptions.

This kind of archaeological reading of the manuscript, in which one interprets aspects of the literary draft such as the 'positioning of the writing on the page', reveals, as Wim Van Mierlo (2013) argues, 'not only the circumstances in which the writing took place, but also the characteristic habits (or *usus scribendi*) of the individual writer' (17). The sketch of Zuleika points to both Beerbohm's visual method of composition and to the primacy – in at least this instance – of the character's graphic representation. But this kind of evidence is dismissed or marginalised even by some genetic critics who continue to privilege word over image. Sally Bushell (2009) does so in evaluating Tennyson's *Morte d'Arthur* manuscripts. In her words, she 'implicitly [took] pictorial representation to be secondary to the written act', in part because of the ways in which Tennyson's drawings (like Beerbohm's) move from being intertwined with the written text in the earliest draft, then pushed to the margin in the second, and excised entirely in later iterations (134). She acknowledges, though, that 'the pictorial element is contributing directly to active composition and helping to release imaginative and creative thought in some way' (134). In the case of Beerbohm's Zuleika sketches, there is a clear if unconfirmed trajectory from Zuleika's pictorial representation and her textual characterisation. The manuscript also suggests more generally that, at least for Beerbohm, the drawing is both the wellspring of the verbal content and an aid to its development. Although we have highlighted the (potential) primacy of drawing for Beerbohm and Tennyson, there are numerous examples of authors for whom drawing played an important if not central role in literary composition. Two examples from non-anglophone writers are Fyodor Dostoevksy (1821–81), whose graphic modes of writing (in which he moves from 'sensory-visual image to literary form') Konstantin Barsht (2016) explores at length (102), and Paul Valery (1871–1945), whose verbal-visual compositional method in *Cahiers* Robert Pickering (1997) defines as 'close to "doodling"' insofar as it is 'removed from any explicitly illustrative intention' (166).

Pickering's reading of Valery's drawing is informative. He refrains from labelling it as doodling because it is undergirded by an 'openness towards an at first unspecified artistic potential which progressively gells to produce a coherent composition' (166). Like Bushell and Barsht, Pickering sees the published and 'coherent' literary work as a terminus that grounds and gives shape to the literary draft and its pictorial content in much the same way that the anticipated final version of a painting conditions teleologically the preliminary sketch. Insofar as an author's pictographic processes are conscious and directed towards the finished literary work, their graphic content could be distinguished from both illustrations and doodles. And, according to Pickering, Valery's method of verbal-visual writing is a deliberate way to articulate what is inexpressible in either language or painting. But doodling is not only a way of complicating and undermining the coherence of the literary manuscript; it is also a way of disrupting fixed meaning in the published text. *Zuleika Dobson*'s avant-textes reveal the role of doodling in textual genesis, but the novel's *après-textes* remind us that the text is never fixed even in its published state.

Eager not to pre-empt readers' visualisations of the novel, Beerbohm (1964) nonetheless reinserted his visual conception of *Zuleika* by creating, as he described it, a 'rather beautiful illustrated and grangerised' version of the book in a 1911 letter to Reggie Turner (212). As he further explained to Turner, he was unsure what he would do with the illustrated edition. He contemplated selling it, and he showed it to friends and family for their amusement, but the book was never sold or published in his lifetime and not until N. John Hall produced a facsimile edition in 1985. Beerbohm described the work as an act of illustration, and indeed many of his gouaches are deliberate and carefully executed illuminations that deploy Kooistra's 'quotation' strategy of illustration. Nevertheless, the illustrated version is more an act of reclamation that recasts the novel as his unique possession and returns the work to its original – more ambiguous and less purely linguistic – form as a decorated manuscript. As Sarah Davison (2011) has argued, *Zuleika*'s publication converted Beerbohm's 'private labor into a public commodity', and the illustrations functioned to 'reclaim the work as his own private masterpiece, effectively returning it to a similar condition of a fair copy' with its own doodles and illustrations (52).

Beerbohm's habit of altering, grangerising, and illustrating books – what he called 'improving' them – was an act of, as Davison (2011) describes, 'interfer[ing] with the signifying apparatus of the book in ways which the authors themselves did not sanction' (58). One notable example that Davison explores is Beerbohm's alterations to his copy of Henry James's *Terminations* (1895). Beerbohm inserts a caricature of James on the book's title page and places in James's mouth a printer's device, an acorn, that gestures towards Beerbohm's rewriting of the collection's first story, 'The Death of the Lion', which centres on the narrator's search for a late author's final literary manuscript. Beerbohm commandeers James's narrative by literally rewriting the story – striking through and inserting new text – supplying a parody version of the missing manuscript and striving to produce a more Jamesian version of the story than even James produced. This type of puckish modification in which Beerbohm not only parodies a text but reauthors it was not restricted to literary works. There are several examples of Beerbohm's 'improving' newspaper photographs and advertisements – such as his careful transformation of the vertical panels of a woman's fur coat into the wooden staves of a basket or barrel in an advertisement for the Lanchester Motor Company (Figure 15). Beerbohm renders this change so skilfully that the transformation is hardly perceptible without juxtaposing it with the original. Working in this mode, Beerbohm is a private graffitist, defacing the works of others where he sees amusement and opportunity and turning the printed text into fodder for a new creation.

Davison (2011) tries to draw a distinction between Beerbohm's interventions into the work of others and his own, describing the former as 'authorially endorsed' (58); however, Beerbohm's post-publication alterations still threaten the stability of the published text regardless of the fact

Figure 15 Max Beerbohm, grangerised advertisement (right) and original (left), 'There's a Car Coming', Lanchester Motor Company (*c.* 1945–6). Merton College Library, Oxford, Beerbohm Collection 8.24. Original artist, Upton Clive (1911–2006). Image courtesy of Merton College Library. Reproduced with permission of the Warden and Fellows of Merton College Oxford and Berlin Associates.

that both word and image derive from Beerbohm's pen. They are in essence *l'esprit de l'escalier*, the embodiment of Beerbohm's afterthoughts and second-guessing. One such drawing is literally *l'esprit de l'escalier* (Figure 16), which makes an appearance in the novel's text as the Duke unsuccessfully searches for a riposte to Zuleika's callous expression of indifference towards him, but which Beerbohm also visually represents as an embodied spirit in his improved copy. Beerbohm is thus not simply reclaiming the text as his own but rather liberating it from the constraints of its published form. In his interventions, Beerbohm resists choices that Heinemann has imposed on the text. For example, to the end-paper advertisement for other Heinemann books Beerbohm adds a self-portrait that asks the reader: 'But perhaps you would rather read one of these.'[20] But he also more generally contests the narrative and semantic closure which that publication represents. He makes reading – even the reading of his own works – a fresh form of authorship that reopens the text, transforms it into a new and still-evolving narrative through a perpetually gestational style of irreverent verbal–visual writing that is best called doodling.

Whether doodling in his manuscripts, grangerising his published works, or defacing adverts in a magazine, Beerbohm is engaged in doodling rather than illustration. He is playing at making and remaking meaning in pictorial form. His book of pastiches, *A Christmas Garland* (1912), is a good example of this practice in verbal form. This play is not inconsequential. In fact, it is essential to the work of authorship and readership, which, as practised by authors, is itself a form of ideation and composition. At its core, literary creation is both laborious and mirthful, but even the hard work of composition produces through its harsh discipline the jovial and spontaneous eruptions that give birth to literary substance. While Beerbohm's doodling has served as an extended example of this practice, it is a habit shared by numerous writers, especially those of the long nineteenth and twentieth centuries when artistic, industrial, and commercial forces aligned to produce the conditions for literary doodling.

[20] For a reproduction of this drawing, see Mercurio and Gabelman 2019, 24, illus. 11.

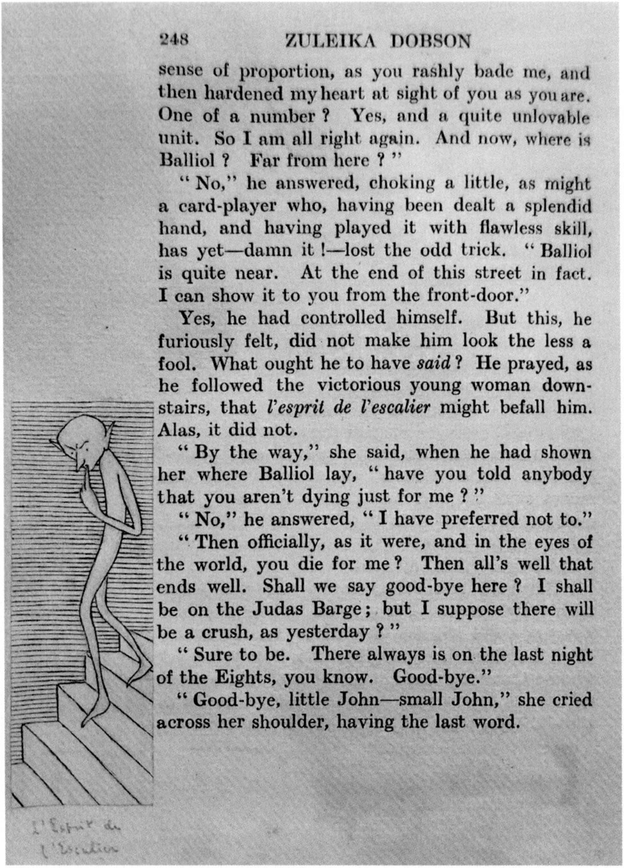

248 ZULEIKA DOBSON

sense of proportion, as you rashly bade me, and then hardened my heart at sight of you as you are. One of a number? Yes, and a quite unlovable unit. So I am all right again. And now, where is Balliol? Far from here?"

"No," he answered, choking a little, as might a card-player who, having been dealt a splendid hand, and having played it with flawless skill, has yet—damn it!—lost the odd trick. "Balliol is quite near. At the end of this street in fact. I can show it to you from the front-door."

Yes, he had controlled himself. But this, he furiously felt, did not make him look the less a fool. What ought he to have *said*? He prayed, as he followed the victorious young woman downstairs, that *l'esprit de l'escalier* might befall him. Alas, it did not.

"By the way," she said, when he had shown her where Balliol lay, "have you told anybody that you aren't dying just for me?"

"No," he answered, "I have preferred not to."

"Then officially, as it were, and in the eyes of the world, you die for me? Then all's well that ends well. Shall we say good-bye here? I shall be on the Judas Barge; but I suppose there will be a crush, as yesterday?"

"Sure to be. There always is on the last night of the Eights, you know. Good-bye."

"Good-bye, little John—small John," she cried across her shoulder, having the last word.

L'Esprit de l'Escalier

Figure 16 Max Beerbohm, 'L'Esprit de l'Escalier', extra-illustration. From grangerised copy of *Zuleika Dobson* (published by Heinemann in 1911), page 248. University of Tulsa, McFarlin Library, Department of Special Collections and University Archives, Sir Rupert Hart-Davis Library, Shelfmark PR6003.E4Z4 1911c RHD. Image courtesy of McFarlin Library, University of Tulsa. Reproduced with permission of Berlin Associates.

EXPLORATION

5 Spectral

Humble yet defiant, doodles dare us to rethink our relationship to texts and ourselves, and they playfully rebel against analytical mastery. The attempt to define doodles and describe their form is by and large a structuralist enterprise, though the fact that we have already had to draw on post-structuralist and post-critical theories points to how resistant doodles are to straightforward structural analysis. Indeed, one of our somewhat paradoxical conclusions from attempting a structuralist approach has been to identify an inescapable phenomenology at the core of doodles – their *effects* and their *affects* both in creators and in viewers. If doodles are at the simplest level – which is already fraught with complexity – playful verbal–visual creations made while the mind is constrained by another activity, then clearly the experience of the doodler is essential. Likewise, the ineluctably playful, ambiguous nature of doodles not only highlights how readers and audiences are always involved in making meaning, but it also necessitates – or at least strongly encourages – a particular type of reader response. This response must be similarly playful, risky, and open to indeterminacy. Many critics balk at this type of reading, either because it does not seem serious or stable enough, or at the opposite end of the spectrum because they venerate the Edenic impenetrability of the doodle. So, on one hand, Michael Camille (1992) explicitly rejects the term 'doodle' as applicable to grotesque marginalia in medieval manuscripts, insisting instead that 'marginal images are conscious usurpations, perhaps even political statements about diffusing the power of the text through its unravelling' (42), while on the other hand, Matthew Battles (2004) sounds almost religious when he 'hesitate[s] to ascribe meaning' to doodles because they 'drop from the Over-soul' and therefore 'their origin is somehow corporate and transpersonal' (108). But readers who refuse to play a more openly active – and more obviously fallible – part in the meaning-making game with doodles can only take their hermeneutical marbles elsewhere.

Building upon the structural/genre insights of the Demarcation part of this Element, we now will consider literary doodling primarily as a mode or impulse, a nexus of certain semiotic tendencies and habits that influences both the creators and readers of literary doodles. This section leans mainly on Derridean deconstruction to explore the eerie spectrality of doodles. In Section 6, we use a variety of psychoanalytic and feminist theorists (Freud, Jung, Kristeva) to delve into their semi-conscious liminality. And Section 7 employs an even more eclectic list of theories and theorists (carnivalesque, nonsense, Gadamer, Frye) to consider how irreducibly ludic doodles are for both creators and readers. By thus turning our critical attention more fully to the phenomenological experience of doodling – as both an act of creation and reception – we hope to understand doodles better on their own irreverent, indeterminate terms.

Encountering a doodle can evoke a sense of the eerie, the uncanny, or even the daemonic. Like handling a holograph from a cherished writer, viewing a doodle can elicit a thrill of psychic intimacy. At times a doodle can feel almost like a medium at a séance channelling the spirit of the dead. Why do doodles exude this unsettling aura? In the rest of this section, we will try to answer this question by tracing the affinities of doodles with the deconstructive thought of Jacques Derrida and close readings of some disturbing doodles in the notebooks of Percy Bysshe Shelley and G. K. Chesterton.

Shelley's doodles have generated more critical writing than almost any other literary doodles (Rogers 1967, Hughes 1970, Goslee 1985, 2011, Allen 2021). In these discussions, doodles are frequently described as eerie, haunting, and even daemonic. Nancy Moore Goslee (1985) notes how 'haunting eyes stare directly out of the notebooks' and how a particular doodle of a cave and island is 'haunting enough' to suggest a link with Demogorgon's cave in Act III of *Prometheus Unbound* (219, 228). Daniel Hughes (1970) claims 'the doodles ... summon the forces deepest in the poem, the psychic clusters lurking in the maze-to-be of language' (201) while Neville Rogers (1967) goes so far as to say of the doodles on a particular page that they 'represent the intrusion into reality, through [Shelley's] pen and pencil, of the daemons that peopled his imagination' (74). As we will see, Shelley's doodles are more unsettling than most; nevertheless, it seems likely that part of what these scholars are experiencing is not unique to Shelley but typical of doodles more generally – their spectrality.

Doodles are unique relics of private psychic phenomena, and, like the relics of religious saints, they seem to hold out the promise of some supertextual revelation to the doodling pilgrim. Yet like relics and ghosts, they lack full incarnation. They are only tentative fragments; hence their interpretations are potentially only figments of the viewer's hermeneutical hopes.

So, in Figure 17 from Shelley's Huntington Notebook No. 2, for example, shadowy half-formed faces compete for physical space and full representational incarnation. Each iteration of the human profile distorts and disfigures the next, in the way noses morph from triangular to bulbous and chins distend from soft to jutting, but also in the way the line of one face transgresses the boundaries of another. Beneath, behind, and within the more prominent ink faces lies a faint, shadowy layer of pencilled faces. A kind of double vision is required to dissolve one image mentally and see through to the even more incorporeal shape beneath. Like ghosts, the images appear to disregard Newtonian and Euclidian laws of matter and space. However, as Goslee (1985) notes, the most 'haunting' features are the eyes, particularly the eternally staring eyes of the faces turned forward creating a simulacrum of something like soul or spirit (219). Meanwhile, on the opposite page (Figure 18) the dark pen outlines of more half-formed faces obscure the faintly pencilled text. The text appears dispossessed – or even possessed – its accustomed centrality on the page usurped by ill-formed phantasms. Gazing through the apparitional figures reveals the draft of a letter Shelley sent to Leigh Hunt relating to his poem about Byron, 'Julian and Maddalo'. Knowing this, one might immediately ask whether any of the doodled faces are attempted representations of Byron or Hunt. While comparisons of the 'haunting eyes' and well-formed lips of the forward-facing doodles with portraits of Hunt are temptingly suggestive, their spectrality denies certainty on this point. For instance, the change of writing implement from pencil to pen could indicate that Shelley doodled these images while transcribing the fair copy that he sent to Hunt (so while thinking of Hunt), or the switch to pen could be the sign of a chronological gap between word and image, suggesting Shelley was just looking for any place to doodle and over

Figure 17 Percy Bysshe Shelley, doodles of faces (*c.* 1819–20) from Huntington Notebook No. 2. (HM 2177), inside back cover. Image courtesy of the Huntington Library, San Marino, California.

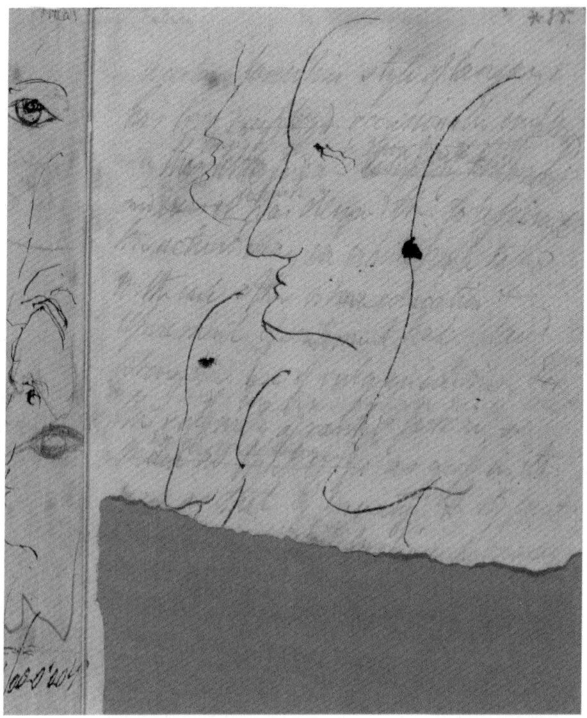

Figure 18 Percy Bysshe Shelley, facial doodles drawn over a draft letter to Leigh Hunt, 1819–20 Huntington Notebook No. 2. HM 2177, backwards page 1 recto. Image courtesy of the Huntington Library, San Marino, California.

a pencilled draft of an already-posted letter was as good a place as any (so nothing to do with Hunt). As with many doodles, a clear link between text and image remains elusive. Nevertheless, Rogers (1967) says that the doodles were the 'intermediaries of [Shelley's] imagination' that informed his textual creations (75). Hughes (1970) adds that they were the 'forms at the *very source* of creative art' and that they reflect 'in an oddly direct and illuminatingly casual way, the poetic process starting below and above words, indicating strange directions and discoveries in the poet's mind' (201) (emphasis original). Likewise, Goslee (2011) claims that Shelley's notebooks are 'partially planned, partially spontaneous, verbal and visual artifacts with their own aesthetic coherence or local coherences – coherences that, once recognized, shape the final versions' and that despite the published versions abandoning the doodles 'traces of that visuality linger in the text' (16). In other words, once one has dwelled with the notebook doodles it is hard not to see their 'traces' in Shelley's texts – they haunt the viewer's imagination and subsequently cast a shadowy presence on his poetry.

In Derrida's (1976) deconstructive philosophy, 'the trace' marks presence with an absence; it is the 'arche-phenomenon of memory' in that it calls into the present an absent event (70). For Shelley, doodling a boat (one of his favourite doodles – see Figure 19) likely invoked memories of sailing and hence a feeling of peace or relaxation – an absent event inscribed into his present that perhaps relieved some psychic tension (boredom, writer's block, anxiety, etc.) or stimulated his imagination. Since Shelley's death in a boating accident, however, viewers of these doodles have found them more chilling and eerie. Introducing 'The Masque of Anarchy' in 1832, Leigh Hunt (1832) gives a description of Shelley's doodling and the effect on Hunt of seeing one of his friend's boat doodles:

> The title-page of the proof is scrawled over with sketches of trees and foliage, which was a habit of his in the intervals of thinking, whenever he had pen or pencil in hand. He would indulge in it while waiting for you at an inn, or in a door-way, scratching his elms and oak-trees on the walls. He did them very spiritedly, and with what the painters call a gusto ... If he had room he would add a cottage, and a piece of water, with a sailing-boat mooring among the trees. This was his *beau ideal* of a life ... What else the image of a boat brings to the memory of those who have lost him, I will not say, especially as he is still with us in his writings. (xiv–xv)

Figure 19 Percy Bysshe Shelley, assorted doodles and sums, 1819–20 Huntington Notebook No. 2. HM 2177, page 1 recto. Image courtesy of the Huntington Library, San Marino, California.

What for Shelley was a *beau ideal* has transformed into a ghostly reminder of his unfortunate death. In Derrida's (1976) sense, the boat doodle is a 'trace', a reminder of 'the nonpresence of the other inscribed within the sense of the present' (71). It is also a trace in the sense that it has become clearly overdetermined; it has eluded or exceeded Shelley's original intention. For Derrida (2001), the trace 'belongs to the very movement of signification' in its 'play of absence and presence' (369). Meaning is created through this playful and uncontrollable movement of presence and absence, which he calls the '(non)logic of play' (Derrida 1981, 158). In 'Spectrographies', Derrida (2002) draws upon ghostly language to describe the same concept:

> What has constantly haunted me in this logic of the spectre is that it regularly exceeds all the oppositions between visible and invisible, sensible and insensible. A spectre is both visible and invisible, both phenomenal and nonphenomenal: a trace that marks the present with its absence in advance. The spectral logic is de facto a deconstructive logic. (117)

The more one looks at doodles (and particularly Shelley's doodles) the more it seems as if there is a kind of 'doodlistic logic' akin to Derrida's '(non)logic of play' and 'spectral logic'.

One of the initial attractions of studying doodles is what Derrida (2001) would call the 'lure of the origin', the logocentric 'dream of deciphering a truth' which 'escapes play and the order of the sign' (372, 369). Doodles awaken a hope of decoding the 'real meaning' of a text or of providing a guarantee of authorial intention in the way that a signature legitimates a document by verifying the identity and intent of its signer. In practice, however, doodles stubbornly refuse to provide the illusion of certainty desired by the logocentric order of things, which is likely one of the reasons they have largely been ignored in critical discourse. Instead, doodles seem peculiarly adept at figuring forth aspects of Derrida's 'trace' and 'spectre': they record highly playful signification-events which not only resist logocentric reduction but also become what Derrida (1981) would term a *pharmakon*, a hermeneutical drug which alternately functions as a medicine and a poison.

We can see something of this happening in Figure 20 where Chesterton intermingles repeated signatures with doodles of William Gladstone and Joseph Chamberlain. A signature, as Derrida (1988) observes, 'implies the actual or empirical nonpresence of the signer' (20). In practice, they culminate letters, officialise legal documents, authorise cheques and bills, or in some other way provide proof of proximity and identity. They are public performances of personal identity. Moreover, in most instances they are singular – three signatures by the same person at the end of a letter would appear farcical and would likely invalidate cheques or legal documents. Here, however, Chesterton excessively reproduces his signature in a kind of autographic bacchanalia. Furthermore, like Shelley's, Chesterton's notebooks were primarily private – they were not intended as public performances. This surfeit of signing thus does not make sense by the normal logic of signatures; it seems instead to belong to the (non)logic of doodles. It is even hard to argue that these are private rehearsals anticipating future public performances in proper autographical contexts – though something of this may be at play – for if this were the case, we could expect to see a reasonable degree of variation, much as an actor in rehearsal might try different gestures, intonations, and expressions. Looking closely at the signatures, though, we find few striking differences that would point to conscious experimentation. Once he adds a looping flourish under the surname rather than the normal straight line, and he alternates how he crosses the 't's between using a single line or two independent lines. All the other changes appear incidental. Taken in isolation, each signature would be considered authentic. In company, however, they deconstruct each other and the ordinary functioning of signature, provoking the question: Which one is in some sense the 'true' or 'essential' signature, or will the real Chesterton please stand up? The doodlistic excess throws into relief 'the impossibility of [a signature's] rigorous purity', for each reiterates the next but always with some – however slight – degree of difference (or *différance* in Derrida's phraseology), thereby exposing and 'haunting' the signature's longing for singularity and identity (Derrida 1988, 20).

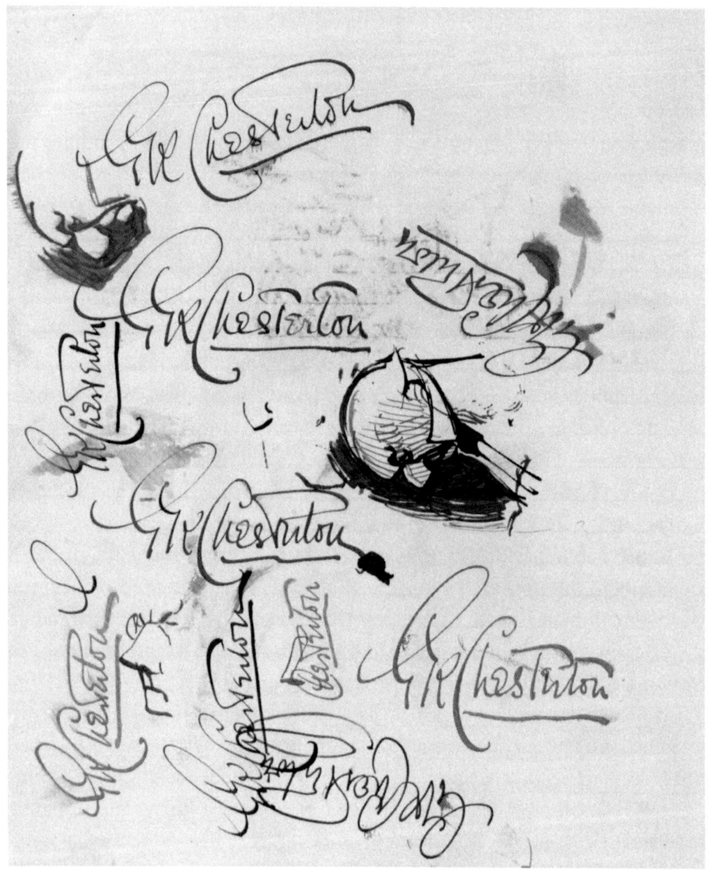

Figure 20 G. K. Chesterton, assorted signatures and doodles (1894–6), BL Add MS 73334, page 18 verso. Image courtesy of the British Library. Reproduced by permission of United Agents Ltd on behalf of the Royal Literary Fund.

The presence of imagistic doodles in, among, and between the signatures also suggests a sort of spectral affinity between signatures and doodles. As a result of habitual repetition, signatures reflect 'an almost entire absence of conscious effort' (Howard 1922, 112). They are the letters, lines, and movements that an individual hand reproduces more than any other in its lifetime. Nor is an individual's signature transferrable to her other hand. It is nearly automatic – it is as though, once summoned, the hand is momentarily possessed by a kinetic daemon. Likewise, doodles seem to have an automatic element: the hand repeatedly echoes lines and figures with which it is habituated as if compelled by an unseen, non-rational force. As already noted, one of Chesterton's daemonic doodling compulsions was the image of Gladstone – particularly his nose. Gladstone's nose materialises incessantly in Chesterton's notebooks with an almost perverse regularity. Chesterton (1900) himself jokes about this obsession in a stanza of his poem 'On the Disastrous Spread of Aestheticism in All Classes':

> But could my kind engross me? No!
> Stern Art – what sons escape her?
> Soon I was drawing Gladstone's nose
> on scraps of blotting paper. (76)

Not surprisingly, the images of Gladstone in the illustration that accompanied this stanza (Figure 21) are almost identical to the ones in Figure 20 (and throughout the notebooks). The hunched artist in the illustration is depicted jotting an army of floating Gladstones in a trance-like doodlistic frenzy, and it is not difficult to imagine Chesterton doing the same in moments when his conscious mind relaxed its bodily command allowing the ghost of Gladstone's nose to reinhabit his susceptible hand. Gladstone's nose is thus in some sense one of Chesterton's 'signature doodles'. Yet the 'logic' of these doodles remains spectral – partially glimpsed because only thinly incarnated.

Doodles are thin because they are incomplete, lacking from their inception a disambiguated teleology. They emerge half-formed from moments of distraction, diversion, or reverie, when the conscious mind temporarily cedes control, allowing unbidden forces to seep through. E. T. A. Hoffmann

Figure 21 G. K. Chesterton, illustration from *Greybeards at Play* (1900), page 77. Public domain. Image from copy held at University of Toronto, available at archive.org.

provides a fictional portrayal of doodling as something eerie, automatic, and quasi-daemonic. In one of the few fictional descriptions of doodling before the 1930s, Hoffmann likely conveys something of his own experiences with doodling, giving us inside access to the perspective of a literary doodler.

In Hoffmann's (2004) 'The Artushof', the protagonist, Herr Traugott, is a bourgeois merchant with artistic aspirations (much like Hoffmann himself from 1796 to 1803) instructed by his business partner to write a formal letter of advice worth ten thousand marks. Sitting at a table in the *Artushof*, a large, busy hall used for commercial transactions (something like an early stock exchange), Traugott begins writing and is 'trying to assemble in his mind the exact wording of his first sentence' when 'he happened to cast his eyes aloft' to the 'strange pictures and carvings with which the walls were hung' (128, 127). Hoffmann depicts the *Artushof* as captured by capitalistic enterprises during the day but with a liminal aesthetic potential, particularly when 'a magical twilight' creeps through the windows, 'inspir[ing]' an 'irresistible' 'urge' to pick up 'paper, pen and ink' to draw these 'strange pictures' (127–8). Succumbing to this 'temptation', Traugott 'instead of getting on with Herr Elias Roos's letter of advice for Hamburg, . . . remained gazing at the marvellous picture and, without thinking what he was doing, began scrawling loops and lines on the paper in front of him' (128–9). Sometime later when his partner asks for the letter, Traugott, 'awakening from his dream' and with 'his mind a blank, handed him the sheet of paper; Herr Roos looked at it, then raised his hands in horror, stamped his foot, and cried: "My God! My God! Scrawlings, childish scrawlings!"' (129–30). Traugott has defaced the important business letter with drawings of two figures from the strange pictures who then mysteriously haunt the remainder of the story. He later discovers among his other drawings one 'he had done in early boyhood which showed, in faltering but nonetheless recognizable outline' the same figures, and he recalls how as a boy 'one evening he had been led as if by an irresistible force away from his games into the Artushof . . . to copy the picture' (137).

In both instances, doodling is a compulsive diversion from some other activity that initiates an eerie reverie and puts Traugott into communion with 'forces' beyond his conscious understanding. The adult experience of the bored businessman has the added element of reconnecting Traugott with something lost or forgotten from his childhood. After gazing on his childhood drawing, Traugott 'was seized by the profoundest sense of sadness and longing' and instead of returning to work for a couple more hours, he gazes 'over the surging sea' and 'endeavoured to descry, as in a magic mirror, the destiny awaiting him' (137). Doodling breaks through the conscious veil of adult seriousness and summons forgotten ghosts of his childhood's deepest desires, and these ghosts haunt Traugott out of the world of business and into an artistic calling. Though dressed in sensational gothic garb, this fictional account likely mirrors something of the catalytic influence of doodling on Hoffmann's own journey from bourgeois clerk to writer, artist, and composer.

Something similarly uncanny and yet far more sinister seems to have happened to G. K. Chesterton during what he called his 'nightmare' at the Slade School of Art. In a chapter in his *Autobiography* called 'How to be a Lunatic', Chesterton ((1937) 1950) recalls how the nihilistic attitudes of some of his fellow decadent art students plunged him into a mood that 'was overpowered and oppressed with a sort of congestion of imagination' and that he 'had an overpowering impulse to record or draw horrible ideas and images' (93). When 'two of his intimate friends' found a notebook 'full of these horrible drawings', they wondered, 'Is Chesterton going mad?' (Ward 1944, 44). Doodles of a devil with an 'evil face' and humans bound in strange positions (e.g., Figure 22) recurred with disturbing regularity, frightening both Chesterton and his close acquaintances (Barker 1973, 50). Doodling was a doorway to his demons: it helped him to 'dig quite low enough to discover the devil; and even in some dim way to recognise the devil' (Chesterton (1937) 1950, 93).

For both creators and viewers, therefore, doodles are haunting. In relinquishing full rational control, doodlers experience a kind of partial possession, as if an alien force momentarily shares control of their hands. Doodles are the traces of this eerie experience. Like the ghosts that are said to bedevil old manor homes because in life they were troubled or had unfinished business, doodles haunt the texts on which they are inscribed as fragmentary and somewhat unsettling (mis)creations. In this way, doodles materialise key principles of Derrida's deconstructive thinking. They play in the gaps between presence and absence, and they resist the logocentric desire for stable meaning and

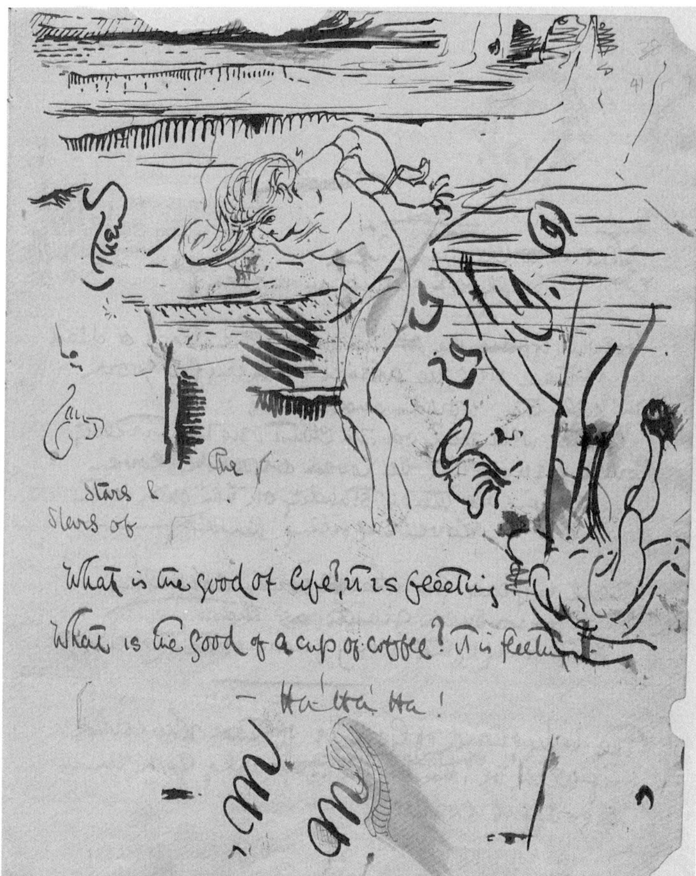

Figure 22 G. K. Chesterton, assorted verbal and visual doodles including a bound human figure (1894–6), BL Add MS 73334, page 41 recto. Image courtesy of the British Library. Reproduced by permission of United Agents Ltd on behalf of the Royal Literary Fund.

interpretative mastery. Looking for authoritative clues, the doodle viewer instead finds a severed sign, which Roland Barthes (1977) calls 'the signifier without the signified' (187). If all we are interested in is hermeneutic certainty, then not only will doodles not help us, but they will also often bewilder our interpretations and frighten us from their habitats. If, however, we are more sympathetic, they might just suggest – tentatively and half-audibly – new insights into the minds of their creators and into our own ways of making meaning.

Traditionally, ghosts are insubstantial phantasms because they are caught between this world and the next. Their transition from life to afterlife remains incomplete; they are suspended in a liminal mode of betwixt and between. Throughout this section, we have seen how doodles inhabit borderlands, fluidly transgressing established boundaries such as those between child/adult, text/image, conscious/unconscious, centre/margin and public/private. In the next section, we will focus on another literary notebook that manifests this type of liminality, and which also happened to be literally haunted.

6 Liminal

In 1787, William Blake's beloved younger brother Robert died of consumption at the age of nineteen. Blake was at the bedside and claimed to see 'the released spirit ascend heavenward through the matter-of-fact ceiling "clapping its hands for joy"' (Gilchrist 1880, 59). Afterwards, he slept for three days and nights in what Peter Ackroyd (1995) calls a 'rite of passage' (99). This tragic event had a lasting impact on Blake and in many ways was a transitional moment that shaped his creative, visionary career. Before Robert's death, Blake had published a collection of juvenile poetry (*Poetical Sketches*, 1783) and a satire (*An Island in the Moon*, 1785) neither of which were illustrated. After Robert's death, Blake discovered the technique of relief etching and enjoyed the most creative period in his life. From 1788 to 1795, Blake produced fourteen of his twenty illuminated manuscripts including *Songs of Innocence and Experience* and *The Marriage of Heaven and Hell*. A catalyst for this transformation seems to have been one of his brother's notebooks, which Blake treasured as 'a continual reminder of [Robert's] living spiritual presence' because it contained his sketches and drawings (Ackroyd 1995, 109). It was in this notebook that Blake began in earnest to develop his unique style of harmonising word and image into a single artistic unity. The notebook might also have been a means of channelling his brother, as in 1788, at a time when he was regularly sketching and jotting in the notebook, Blake claimed that his brother appeared to him in a vision and revealed the method of relief etching that he subsequently used for all his illuminated books.

Whatever one makes of Blake's unorthodox claims, it seems probable that he was experiencing what psychoanalysts and anthropologists would call a 'liminal period' in his life. Following Arnold van Gennep, Victor Turner (1979) defines liminality as an 'interstructural situation' between established cultural positions characteristic of transitional moments such as 'birth, puberty, marriage, and death' (226). These 'rites of passage' are fundamentally ambiguous; they unhinge identity, creating a 'liminal *persona*' that is neither one thing nor another: 'liminal entities are neither here nor there; they are betwixt and between the positions assigned and arrayed by law, custom, convention, and ceremonial' (Turner 1977, 95). Although liminality is thus uncertain and insecure, it is also profoundly liberated. It is in some ways 'a stage of reflection' and a 'realm of primitive hypothesis, where there is a certain freedom to juggle with the factors of existence' (Turner 1979, 226).

This liminal freedom to play with elemental reality perhaps helps to explain why Blake's first project in the notebook after Robert's death is 'Ideas of Good and Evil' and why the early sketches often depict death, travellers, and mercurial beings. Peter Ackroyd (1995) observes how the 'depictions of sickness and fatality, of floating spirits and figures upon clouds' gesture to the way in which 'the experience of Robert's death had infused the notebook' (109). Yet at the same time, 'in the margins Blake also doodled some more mundane scenes' such as 'a man urinating against a wall, a boy and a dog looking at each other intently, a monstrous figure swooping down from the skies like some harbinger of moral decay' (109). Here Ackroyd refers to a page in the notebook (Figure 23) in which the central emblem of a traveller and the lightly pencilled inscription, 'Thus the traveller hasteth in the Evening', are surrounded and infringed upon by an odd array of unframed, unfinished 'doodled' images. The central framed and inscribed image is the authorial intention for the page and, though still sketch-like, is the most finished. It conforms to established literary and artistic conventions and is purposed for publication. The doodles, meanwhile, are marginal and liminal: they are in a kind of 'interstructural situation' disconnected from distinct intentionality and therefore more liberated to play thematically and stylistically. A close look at the figure in the top left corner suggests not only that he is urinating but that he is also the traveller from the emblem. The metaphysical seriousness of the traveller as a symbol of life and spiritual journeying is thus debased in a Rabelaisian manner. Similarly, the staring man and dog at the bottom left could be seen as further undermining the philosophical solemnity of the traveller in the light-hearted linking of human and animal. Meanwhile, on the upper right side, the thrice repeated figure of a spectral monster carrying a lifeless body in its jaws appears to threaten the traveller with his ultimate fate. Taken together, the doodles seem 'to juggle with the factors of existence' riffing off the page's 'official' theme in an uncensored, unrestricted manner.

Figure 23 William Blake, 'Emblem: the traveller hasteth in the evening' (1787–9), Notebook of William Blake, BL Add 49460, f.9. Image courtesy of the British Library.

Moreover, the relationship between the doodles and the central emblem is parodic and non-reciprocal. The conventionality of the frame shelters the traveller from the threats to his *telos* and signals the fixedness of his essence. The doodles, however, lack the security and clarity of borders. Like their marginal positions on the page, their meaning as doodles hangs tenuously and precariously off the sanctioned central 'text'. In the absence of the doodles the emblem would retain its primary meaning, but in the absence of the emblem the doodles would lose essential aspects of their signification. The figure in the top left corner, for instance, would lose his inverted mirroring function and become merely a urinating man. In this way, doodles are potentially parasitic, much in the same way that parody is dependent upon what it mocks. As liminal entities they are in some sense constituted by that which they are not.

A further aspect of the liminality of doodles is their ambiguous relationship to both consciousness and the unconscious. According to Jung (1976), 'the unconscious contains all the fantasy combinations which have not yet attained the threshold intensity' while 'consciousness, because of its directed functions, exercises an inhibition on all incompatible material, with the result that it sinks into the unconscious' (274). In normal people, the boundary between the two is 'stable and definite' but in certain individuals – neurotics and creative artists – the 'partition between conscious and unconscious is much more permeable' (275). This description aptly characterises Blake, both as artist and potential neurotic. Looking again at Figure 23, the emblem seems to display more of the 'directed functions' of consciousness while the doodles seem to portray 'fantasy combinations' of the unconscious. The frame excludes and censors the other riotous images from the 'stable and definite' meaning of the emblem, thereby preparing the way for publication – the ultimate creative 'threshold intensity'. The doodles, on the other hand, are much closer to the logic of dreams and free association: tangential, tendentious, and anarchic.

According to Freud (1921), dreams are a product of 'the primary process', the primitive method which the unconscious uses to release the tension built up by the id's constant striving after the pleasure principle. The primary process is preverbal and therefore mainly visual. Desires that are constantly repeated but not fulfilled create images in the unconscious, and these images serve to discharge some of the psychic tension resulting from lack of fulfilment. As a result of constant repetition and whimsical free association, the images undergo condensation and compromise until they are 'endowed with marked intensity', which allows them to rise to the threshold of consciousness and manifest in dreams (197). When sleep forces the ego to relinquish its psychic dominance, the primary process takes over and dreaming reigns. At other times, however, the ego engages the primary process for its own purposes. So jokes intentionally – though not necessarily consciously – condense and distort language in a way that bypasses the moral and conventional restraints of the superego. Consequently, the 'pleasure [of jokes] arises from an economy in psychical expenditure or a relief from the compulsion of criticism' (Freud 1963, 127).

From this Freudian perspective, doodles are products of the primary process that help to release psychic tension through relaxing inhibitions and purging troublesome mental images. Doodling can be a psychic aid during more serious activities because, according to E. H. Gombrich (1999), 'it requires no concentration, but it keeps our minds busy and amused' (224). In particular, it can prevent the doodler from dwelling on distracting ideas: 'fantasises and thoughts hidden in doodles are those of which the doodler wants to liberate himself' (222). For professional artists, doodles also circumvent the 'strict discipline' and 'rigid formulas' of artistic convention, allowing the pleasure of play to predominate and opening up new representational possibilities (215).

In Blake's notebook, doodles thus seem to play with both form and meaning in an anarchic, unsettling manner, perhaps reflecting Blake's attempts to liberate himself from the psychic tension created by his visions and fantasies. Like Figure 23, Figure 24 has a central framed and inscribed emblem that is being infringed upon by various elements. A quotation from Milton's poem 'On the Death of a Fair Infant' gives clarity and fixedness to the image of a woman cradling a small bundle in her arms: 'Yet can I not perswade me. Thou art dead.' Above, the dark penned lines of an epigram questions the goodness and authority of God: 'To God / If you have formed a Circle to go into / Go into it yourself & see how you would do.' Meanwhile three flying creatures hover around the mourning woman much in the same way that the flying monsters in Figure 23 infringe upon and

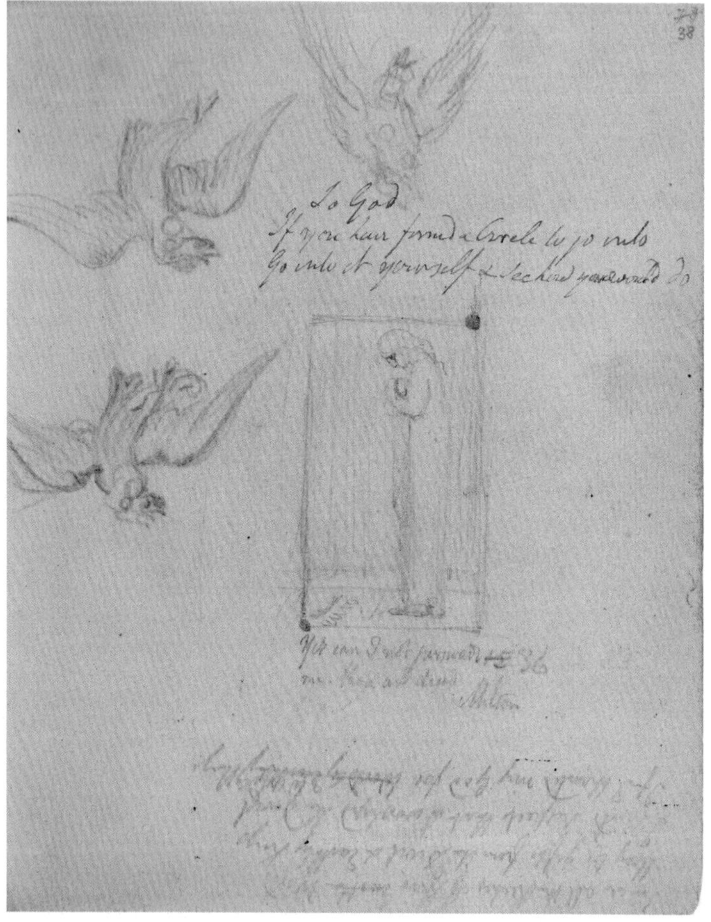

Figure 24 William Blake, 'Emblem 48; mother and dead child' (1787–9), Notebook of William Blake, BL Add 49460, f.38. Image courtesy of the British Library.

threaten the traveller. In both cases, one image is repeated three times, condensing and intensifying its significance, much as the primary process imparts threshold intensity to dreams through condensation and free association. Both flying creatures are related to death, but in Figure 23, the doodles are more sinister and menacing. The corpse-filled maw and massive staring eyes of the hairy humanoid face seem to channel the terror of death. On the other hand, the feathered birdlike creature on Figure 24 seems more beneficent; the figures it carries – possibly the mother and child from the emblem – cling to its neck and merge fluidly into its form. Rather than terror, the images evoke hope almost as if to comfort the woman forever fixed in her grief. Having relaxed the ego's compulsion for completion, however, the doodles remain open, unsettled, and ambiguous; they are positioned between conscious creations intended for public consumption and the purely private dream-works of the unconscious.

This liminality also partially explains why doodles are sometimes seen as embarrassing – they can manifest parts of the psyche that consciousness normally censors before presenting to others. On top of this, the rough, careless style of many doodles might seem beneath the dignity of artists capable of skilful, serious creations. Liminal entities are embarrassing because they threaten the semiotic order of things. Kristeva (1982) describes this as a state of 'abjection'. That which 'does not respect borders, positions, rules' disturbs 'identity, system, order' (4). To protect the social aggregate 'defilement [must be] jettisoned from the "*symbolic system*"' (65) (emphasis original). Similarly, doodles are also readily jettisoned in the creative process – erased, overwritten, discarded, crossed out, or destroyed – partially because they are spectral and not invested with full teleology, but partially because their presence near authorised 'texts' endangers the order of signification much as homeless tramps threaten the pristine logic of the capitalist marketplace. For example, Max Beerbohm frequently scribbled over the doodles in his earliest manuscript of *Zuleika Dobson* (Figure 14) as if embarrassed by their execution, by what they potentially signified, or perhaps by the act of doodling itself as a digression from the designated activity of novel writing. Crossing out is thus a clear sign of self-censorship. The doodler, in a kind of half-conscious, liminal state, suspends criticism and ignores aspects of social, artistic, or literary conventions, but the return of single-mindedness also brings critical awareness and embarrassment. Significantly, there are no doodles in the later manuscript of *Zuleika Dobson*, suggesting that rewriting for Beerbohm was akin to the single-mindedness of criticism while early drafting provided more space for creative free play. Beerbohm allowed himself to doodle during the work's genesis much as parents allow children to play during youth. However, as the work matured, Beerbohm curtailed his raucous play, sanitising the text of embarrassing things that might threaten the novel's 'symbolic system'.

The liminality of doodles – being 'betwixt and between', neither this nor that – can thus be embarrassing because of their potential for revealing the psyche in unguarded, uncensored moments. In addition, the liminal ambiguity of doodles also points to their love of pleasure and play.

7 Ludic

Deriving from the German *Dödel* meaning a fool or simpleton, the word 'doodle' before the 1930s denoted 'a silly or foolish fellow' (*OED*). Richard Cobden (1872), for instance, deridingly refers to the 'Noodles and Doodles of the aristocracy', and British soldiers during the French and Indian War famously mocked the ridiculous naiveté of Americans in 'Yankee Doodle' (quoted in *OED*). One reason why the word became attached with 'aimless scrawls' made while the mind is 'otherwise applied' is thus undoubtedly embarrassment of the foolishness of drawings created in a liminal state. Perhaps a more primal reason, though, is the oral, aural, and visual pleasure that the word can unconsciously evoke. The consonants and vowels in 'doodle' are simple and unsophisticated, corresponding to some of the earliest sounds that a baby can make. The 'oo' sound is suggestive of how babies coo when happy, while the reiteration of the easy to pronounce 'd' sound recalls the infant pleasure in babble and repetition as seen in the earliest English words: mama, dada, papa, boo-boo. In short, doodle is a fun word to say and to hear.

It is also fun to see and to write. Comprised of a simple series of circles and vertical lines, the word 'doodle' could be seen as a visual instantiation of what it signifies. The long, straight vertical lines are swift and emphatic. The endless curvature of the circles is mesmerising, and the final 'e' could be viewed either as a kind of flourish or as an unfinished circle. Jean-Luc Nancy (2013) argues that 'the first person who drew on a rock face a deer . . . or a sinuous line opened the door to an endlessly modulated repetition of his gesture' and that 'this repetition . . . nurtures a pleasure whose essence is repetition itself' (26). The simple repetition with variation of elemental shapes such as circles and vertical lines is a primal pleasure, one commonly known as play.

Johan Huizinga's ((1944) 2007) *Homo Ludens* gives another early meta-discursive description of doodling that identifies play as a central characteristic:

> An almost instinctive, spontaneous need to decorate things cannot, indeed, be denied; and it may conveniently be called

> a play-function. It is known to everybody who, pencil in hand, has ever had to attend a tedious board meeting. Heedlessly, barely conscious of what we are doing, we play with lines and planes, curves and masses, and from this abstracted doodling emerge fantastic arabesques, strange animals and human forms. We may leave it to the psychologists to attribute what unconscious 'drives' they will to this supreme art of boredom and inanition. But it cannot be doubted that it is a play-function of low order akin to the child's playing in the first years of its life, when the higher structure of organised play is as yet undeveloped. (168)

Huizinga's comments support much of what we have already discussed about the nature of doodles. They are 'spontaneous' and 'instinctive', manifesting as 'fantastic arabesques, strange animals and human forms' almost as if, lured by pencil and mental distraction, a kinaesthetic daemon temporarily possesses the hand, producing spectral, unfinished forms. They are also 'half-conscious' liminal creations springing from 'unconscious drives' that hover in the borderland between public and private. However, Huizinga also draws attention to how doodles are the 'supreme art of boredom and inanition' and 'akin to the child's playing in the first years of its life'. Examining this interstice between play and boredom, therefore, might further help to elucidate literary doodling.

In 1830, at the age of eighteen, Edward Lear began visiting the Zoological Gardens to make drawings of parrots for his first book, *Illustrations of the Family of the Psittacidae, or Parrots*. For twelve months, he 'moved, thought, looked at & existed among Parrots' (Lear 1988, 16). Boredom under such circumstances was probably inevitable, and one of the ways he alleviated the tedium of measuring wingspans and counting tail feathers was doodling human visitors and other animals. Vivien Noakes (2004) observes: 'Sitting in the parrot house he was obviously regarded as something of a curiosity himself, for the visitors came and stared at him and his work and, as a change from drawing birds, he would make indignant, Doyle-like sketches of the bonneted ladies and startled gentlemen who peered at him' (17). Most of the pages that remain from this period depict a single meticulously drawn parrot at their centre. A few, however, portray a skilfully sketched central parrot surrounded by more lightly pencilled, unfinished doodles.

Figure 25, for example, has a parrot perched on a branch with its head bent downwards in a posture that Lear used for his final illustrations of both the parakeet and the macaw. As in William Blake's notebook (Figures 23 and 24), this sanctioned, fully intentional sketch is being encroached upon by playful doodles that subvert the single-minded purpose of sketching publishable parrots. Monotony, though, is the breeding ground for boredom. The strain of fixing one's entire attention on a single object for long stretches can drain mental energy and leave a feeling of emptiness symptomatic of boredom.

At least as far back as the book of Ecclesiastes, writers have commented on how burdensome an experience of emptiness can be: 'vanity of vanities! All is vanity!' (1:2). Noting the surprisingly late emergence in English of the words 'bore' (1780) and 'boredom' (1852), however, Patricia Spacks (1976) wryly comments that 'if people felt bored before the late eighteenth century, they didn't know it' (14). Modern boredom seems to have arisen from the same phenomena that gave rise to literary doodling (bourgeois culture, school, the inward turn, industrial production, and consumption).[21] Peter Toohey (2011) defines it as 'an emotion which produces feelings of being constrained or confined by some unavoidable and distastefully predictable circumstance and, as a result, a feeling of being distanced from one's surroundings and the normal flow of time' (45).

There are two stereotypical examples of boredom and doodling in the memoir of Henry Liddell, perhaps most famous today as the father of Alice Liddell of *Alice in Wonderland*, but also one of the greatest classical scholars of his day and dean of Christ Church, Oxford. Liddell was a lifelong doodler, who, like most of his fellow nineteenth-century doodlers, learned the habit at school while being constrained to learn Latin and Greek. Even Liddell, who went on to co-author the subsequently infamous *Liddell & Scott Greek–English Lexicon* that made schoolboys like Aldous Huxley ache

[21] For more on literary doodling as a nineteenth-century cultural phenomenon, see our companion volume *Literary Doodling in Britain, 1789–1930* (forthcoming).

Figure 25 Edward Lear, 'Parrot and sketches of human figures' (1832), MS Typ 55.9 (60), Houghton Library. Image courtesy of Houghton Library, Harvard University.

with 'ennui',[22] found his classical education tedious at times, particularly when 'it was [his] lot to sit next to W. Makepeace Thackeray' (Thompson 1899, 8). Rather than 'grapple with the Horace', the two 'spent [their] time mostly in drawing' things such as 'comic scenes' and 'burlesque representations of incidents in Shakespeare' (Thompson 1899, 8). Yet boredom is not unique to schools. As chairman of the governing body of Christ Church, Liddell often battled ennui with the sword of doodling:

> He was very patient of tedious speakers, and would solace himself by taking out his gold pen, and ... would draw wondrous landscapes on the pink blotting paper which lay before him, while the stream of talk flowed on. Churches, castles, bridges, ruined keeps, and ivy-clad walls, woodland and river scenes, in endless variety, were the outcome of dreary sessions of the innumerable committees which Oxford crowds into the afternoons of its all too brief Terms. Many hundred sketches from his pen are still treasured up by his friends; he would leave them on the table at the end of a meeting. (Thompson 1899, 194–95)

One surviving doodle from these meetings seems clearly to convey Liddell's 'feelings of being constrained or confined by some unavoidable and distastefully predictable circumstance', as Toohey (2011) describes boredom. In Figure 26, a bald man depicted from behind (Liddell was bald) looks towards a closed, narrow window which tantalises with the prospect of freedom while remaining distant and inaccessible. Windows are inherently liminal structures granting visual access even as they deny physical access, and this window seems particularly suited to a cell. Doodling was Liddell's window of 'solace' during the imprisoning tedium. Or to put it the other way round, boredom was his stimulus to doodle.

22 'Even today the sight of ... Liddell's and Scott's *Greek Lexicon*, has power to recall that ancient ennui. What dreary hours I have spent frantically turning those pages in search of a word for "cow" that could be scanned as a dactyl' (Huxley 1955, 44).

Figure 26 Henry Liddell, doodle of a bald man looking towards a narrow window, Christ Church Henry Liddell-doodles. Image courtesy of Christ Church, University of Oxford.

It is important to note that doodling does not eliminate boredom. The best remedy for boredom, as Toohey (2011) points out, is probably 'to walk away from the situation that is provoking it' (174). By the definition we are setting out, though, doodling occurs only when an individual is in some sense 'constrained and confined' by another task, purpose, or circumstance. These constraints are often self-imposed – as with Lear trapping himself with parrots for a year – but they are not therefore less onerous. Indeed, the superego can be a much crueller taskmaster than any teacher or employer.

Being confined by another task or circumstance, however, does not necessarily entail boredom or even psychic discomfort. Battles's (2004, 107) claim that doodles are the 'graphic expression of ennui' seems true in many circumstances, but it does not apply universally and is impossible to determine definitively. Freud, for instance, doodled at meetings of the Vienna 'Psychological Wednesday Society', a club he formed for intellectual and social companionship and held at his house, and while this habit may have been prompted by particularly boring papers or conversations, it seems at least equally as likely that his doodles are traces of his attention to the proceedings rather than his inattention (Freud, Freud, and Grubrich-Simitis 1978, 181). Recent psychological studies argue that doodling might participate in 'an anatomically distinct neuronal network', one which when active leads to 'a simultaneous reduction in the activity of another neuronal network, i.e., the "attention system" (which is activated for goal directed thought)' (Gupta 2016, 17). Doodling also seems to enhance short-term working memory for auditory information – though not for visual information, which likely competes for the same neural processing power – paradoxically heightening attention through apparent inattention (Andrade 2010).

Doodling in contexts where the primary medium of confinement is auditory – classrooms, lectures, sermons, poetry readings – might, therefore, be a sign of engagement or even enjoyment rather than boredom. One such example might be Dante Gabriel Rossetti's doodles of George MacDonald and several unidentified female figures done on the back of a programme advertising 'Lectures by Mr George MacDonald' on Chaucer, Shakespeare, and Tennyson (Figure 28). MacDonald was an extremely popular and respected lecturer and preacher known for his engaging extemporaneous style. Almost all MacDonald's lectures and sermons were done without notes. MacDonald was also an acquaintance of Rossetti's, and the subject of the lecture – whichever of the three Rossetti attended – would have been one of interest to him. Moreover, unlike the lectures that university students are forced to sit through, Rossetti would have been under no compulsion to attend. Hence, the contexts make it seem probable that Rossetti enjoyed the lecture.

Close readings of the doodles point in this direction as well. All the doodles seem to have been done with the same implement (fountain pen with brown ink) in one sitting, but there seems to have been a progression from rough and desultory to more polished and attentive. The half-formed female profiles on the back of the programme in Figure 28 seem to have preceded both the image of MacDonald and the more refined female figure on the front of the programme in Figure 27. This is because at least one profile has been subsumed in MacDonald's hair while several more have been scratched through either in an act of self-censorship (erasing the embarrassing origins of the refined female doodle) or to focus attention on the MacDonald doodle (or both). One could imagine Rossetti amusing himself either while waiting for the lecture to begin or in its early stages by idly doodling the profile of a woman – either in the crowd or one of his models from memory – and, after several half-hearted, aborted attempts, turning the programme over to formulate a more finished drawing with careful hatching and more assured lineation – a marked evolution from the rudimentary shapes on the back.[23] Counter-intuitively, though, this increased attention to visual detail could reflect a simultaneous increase in attention to auditory information. This might be supported by the supposition that Rossetti then seems to have shifted his doodling focus to the lecturer himself as if the voice drew him irresistibly to the face. As he became more absorbed in the oration and topic, he might have become more graphically stimulated. Had he been merely bored, this would have been more likely to express itself in the mock aggression of caricature (like Lear) or the weary uninterest of escapism (like Liddell). Instead, Rossetti's

[23] Given the frequency with which he sketched beautiful women, feminine profiles might have been nearly as automatic for Rossetti as Gladstone's nose was for Chesterton.

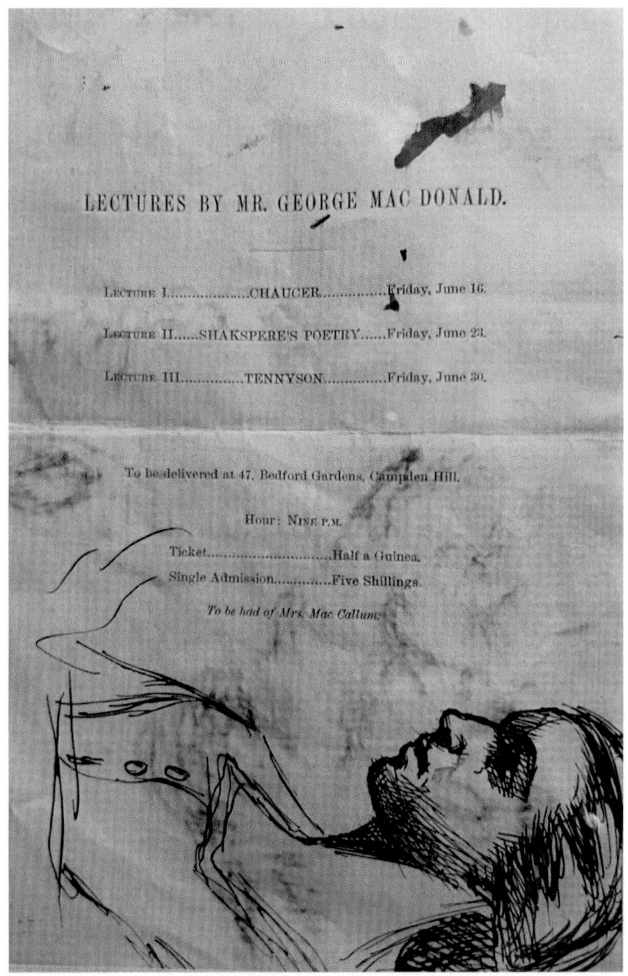

LECTURES BY MR. GEORGE MAC DONALD.

LECTURE I...................CHAUCER...............Friday, June 16.

LECTURE II......SHAKSPERE'S POETRY......Friday, June 23.

LECTURE III...............TENNYSON...............Friday, June 30.

To be delivered at 47, Bedford Gardens, Campden Hill.

Hour: NINE P.M.

Ticket..............................Half a Guinea.

Single Admission.............Five Shillings.

To be had of Mrs. Mac Callum.

Figure 27 Dante Gabriel Rossetti, doodle of a woman (half-length) on a programme advertising lectures by George MacDonald, private collection. Image courtesy of Christopher MacDonald.

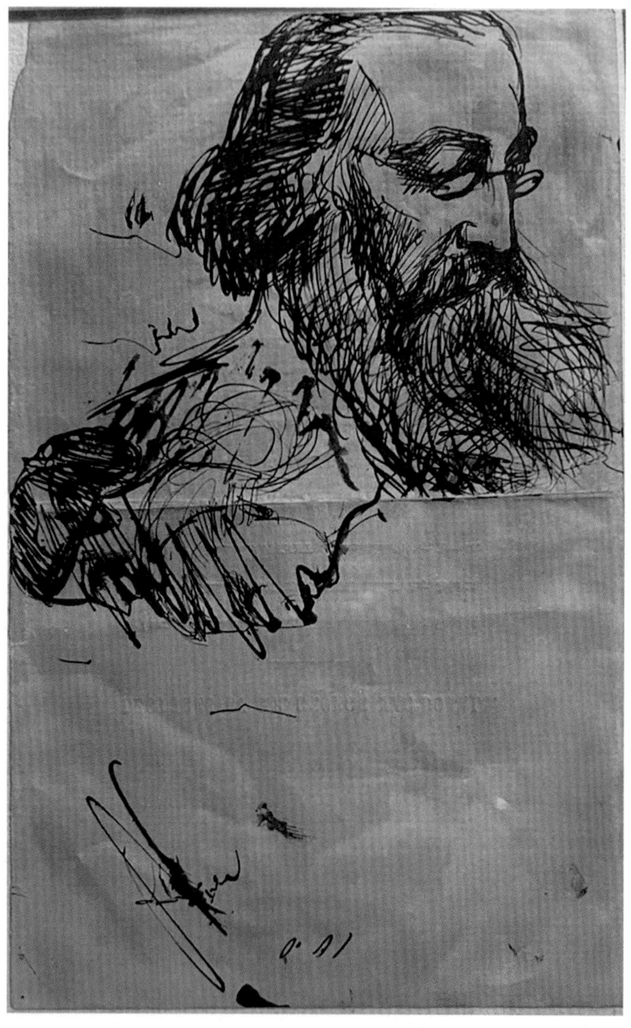

Figure 28 Dante Gabriel Rossetti, doodle of George MacDonald lecturing with doodles of women in profile, private collection. Image courtesy of Christopher MacDonald.

doodling became keener and more sensitive to its subject. The doodle of MacDonald delicately balances the calm, deep wisdom of his large forehead and bespectacled eyes with the anarchic dynamism of the hairs in his unruly beard – the gravitas of the scholar with the untamed passion of the preacher. There is no mockery discernible in the doodle, only admiration, suggesting that Rossetti was fully arrested by the lecture, not just by MacDonald's ideas but by his personality and powers of wise yet forceful expression.

It is, therefore, possible for doodling to be an aid to attention, particularly in auditory contexts where the visuality of doodling does not compete for the same neuronal resources, but in Edward Lear's parrot house this was not possible because his task was entirely visual. In most cases, in fact, doodling seems to relax and even subvert the seriousness constraining the individual. Gombrich (1999) argues that 'it is only when [artistic] standards are deliberately loosened that artistic practice becomes permeable to that free play of the pen we call doodling' (215). So, in Figure 25, Lear has painstakingly drawn the parrot in a naturalistic style with every claw and feather precisely imitating the living bird, but the human figures are hastily sketched with fewer, lighter lines in the style of grotesque caricature popularised at the time by John Doyle and George Cruikshank. The three figures at the bottom of the page are comically out of proportion, accentuated by exaggerations such as plumes that are longer than legs. The face in the top right corner, meanwhile, is laughably contorted with bent and jagged lines and oddly misshapen eyes, nose, and mouth. Perhaps most humorous of all is the portly bald man who seems to be blithely engaged in a staring match with the parrot. The connected gaze of the two images draws them into a shared realm where the unconcerned cartoon man stands precariously near the monstrous, oversized, and rather voracious-looking parrot. The light-hearted play here subverts Lear's intended aim of rigid naturalism, likely providing temporary relief from the tedium of studying the family Psittacidae.

Lear's whimsical drawings also gesture towards the affinity of doodling with another playful mode: the grotesque. According to Mikhail Bakhtin's (1984) theory of carnival, the grotesque functions through 'degradation and debasement'. It lowers the lofty, breaks down the monolithic, and frees laughter from the chains of seriousness. The grotesque 'liberates man from all the forms of in-human necessity that direct the prevailing concept of the world' and in this way 'frees human consciousness, thought, and imagination for new potentialities' (49). Techniques such as exaggeration, inversion, excess, estrangement, and the juxtaposition of high and low help to release laughter, and 'laughter liberates not only from external censorship but first of all from the great interior censor' (94). Similarly, Lear's doodling in the parrot house liberatingly draws upon exaggeration, excess, and discordant juxtaposition, not only bringing him temporary relief from boredom but also seemingly opening up vital creative avenues that Lear was to explore in later life in his nonsense.

John Ruskin (1856–60) describes a related aspect of the grotesque in *Modern Painters* when he says how 'the playful grotesque' (one of three types he identifies) arises 'from healthful but irrational play of the imagination in times of rest' (3:97). Coleridge ((1817) 2000) would likely have called this 'fancy' rather than 'imagination' because there is an element of passivity involved and fancy is 'always the ape' (473). Aping something is restful and passive because it does not require great creative effort – it is light, easy, and seemingly automatic. In this way, it is closer to the play of children than to the more sophisticated, formal play of art, literature, and beauty. 'The ease of play', as Hans-Georg Gadamer (2006) points out, 'is experienced subjectively as relaxation' for 'the structure of play absorbs the player into itself, and thus frees him from the burden of taking the initiative, which constitutes the actual strain of existence' (105). More so than adults, children delight in the primal joy of repetition – the thrill of mastery that comes from effortlessly performing a hard-won skill and the pleasure of reliving positive moments. Whereas adults are 'goal-oriented' and 'purpose driven', children are more interested in play as 'to-and-fro movement that is not tied to any goal that would bring it to an end' (104). Doodles, as we have already seen, lack clear teleology, but they also revel in repetition and the relaxation of eschewing 'the burden of taking the initiative'. It should perhaps not be surprising, then, that Lear incorporated so many birds and parrots into his doodlistic nonsense drawings. After a year of intensive study, drawing parrots became easy, pleasurable, and automatic.

At the bottom of his holograph manuscript of 'The Scroobious Pip', for example, Lear has sketched four images of the fantastical creature (Figure 29).

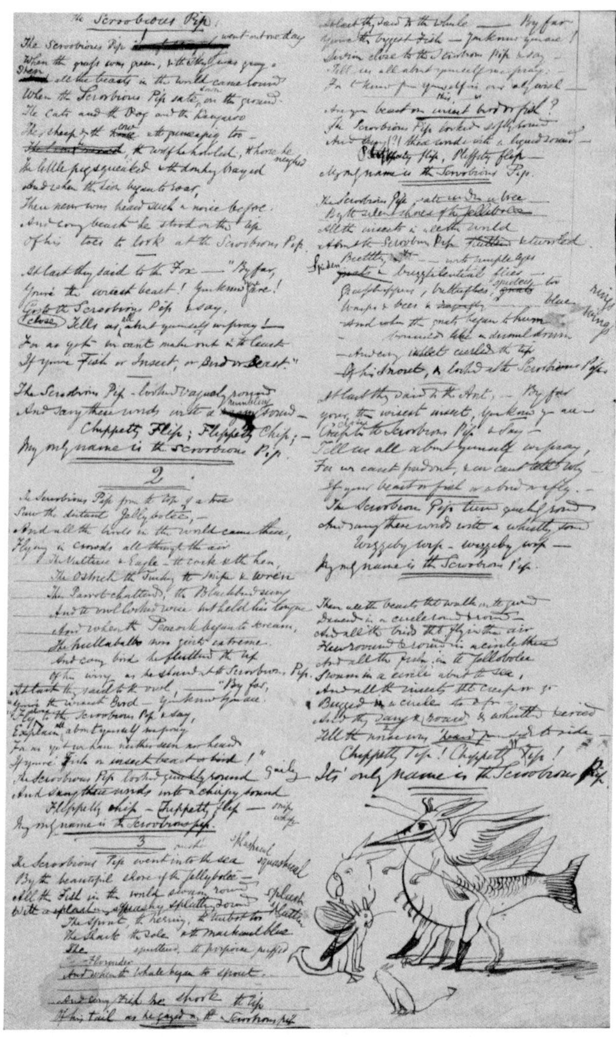

Figure 29 Edward Lear's holograph of 'The Scroobious Pip' with doodlistic images. MS Typ 55.14 (159 R), Houghton Library. Image courtesy of Houghton Library, Harvard University.

The largest, most finished figure is a kind of portmanteau animal with a scaly fish tail, feathered wings, antennae, multiple clawlike hands, and five booted legs. Undoubtedly this is a creation of fancy and the playful grotesque in its random association of disparate elements. The three other images, however, are distinctly parrot-like and appear, from their simplicity and incompleteness, to precede the more detailed image. The joy of repeating the familiar shape seems to have compelled Lear's half-conscious mind in these initial forms; upon more conscious reflection, though, he discarded the parrot's curved beak in favour of grotesque excess. It is likely that had Lear finished and published this poem, he would have included something very similar to the larger image with the nonsense poem (as Ogden Nash did when the poem was published posthumously). This probable intention makes it difficult to classify the images definitively as doodles; nonetheless, there is something undeniably doodlistic about all of Lear's nonsense – poetry and illustration. Compared to Lewis Carroll's *Alice* stories and Tenniel's illustrations, for instance, Lear's nonsense books come across as less fraught with intentionality and containing more of the uncomplicated play of the child. The limericks in particular with their habitual repetition of poetic form, common themes, and crude, sparse style are more akin to 'to-and-fro movement that is not tied to any goal' than the carefully plotted chess narrative and complex dialogues of *Alice Through the Looking Glass*. Moreover, the brevity of the limericks means that everything exists in a spectral way – nothing is resolved or given full embodiment – and psychoanalytic critics have long noted the latent content in Lear's liminal creations. Therefore, it seems as if doodling also has affinities with nonsense literature (particularly Lear's less calculated brand of nonsense).

In *Anatomy of Nonsense*, Wim Tigges (1988) claims that nonsense has four essential characteristics: 'an unresolved tension between presence and absence of meaning, lack of emotional involvement, playlike presentation, and an emphasis, stronger than in any other type of literature, upon its verbal nature' (55). As we have seen, the first three essential characteristics of nonsense could also apply to doodling, suggesting that the main difference between nonsense and doodling might just be the medium of their play – verbal and visual, or 'babble' and 'doodle' to use Northrop Frye's terms (1990, 278). Both 'babble' and 'doodle', Frye tells us, draw upon 'subconscious association' to spawn their creations (275). Nonsense thus relies heavily on puns, rhyme, assonance, alliteration, portmanteaus, and neologisms to guide its formation. So, Chesterton (1900), in his nonsense poem 'On the Disastrous Spread of Aestheticism in All Classes', writes:

> Then on – to play one-fingered tunes
> Upon my aunt's piano,
> In short, I have a headlong soul,
> I much resemble Hanno.
>
> (Forgive the entrance of the not
> Too cogent Carthaginian
> It may have been to make a rhyme;
> I lean to that opinion.) (80)

Here Chesterton parenthetically acknowledges the formative impact of the babble impulse on the poem. Phonic similarity is not considered a sophisticated principle of logical or narrative ordering, but it is part of the way minds function linguistically. Thus, the aural association of 'piano' and 'Hanno' forces the poet to progress in a suprising, disjointed direction. Driven by subconscious association, the nonsense writer is also not in full control of his writing and feels – with a heavy dose of irony – obliged to apologise for a particularly egregious digression, though he is still unable to say definitively why he did it ('I lean to that opinion') as if distant and detached from his own creation. The nonsense writer playfully embraces and exagerates the way that words, as Derrida (1976) observes, always express 'more, less, or something other than what [we] mean' (158). Nonsense removes the illusion that we are masters of words, instead highlighting the extent to which we are always governed by language. As Lecercle (1994) puts it, 'it is language that speaks: I am constrained by the language I inhabit to such an extent that I am inhabited, or possessed by it' (25). Chesterton's haunted 'babble' then leads to digressive 'doodle' as he illustrates the stanza (Figure 30) with the dandified speaker posing beside a monstrous, menancing Hanno.

Figure 30 G. K. Chesterton, illustration to 'On the Disastrous Spread of Aestheticism in All Classes', *Greybeards at Play* (1900), page 81. Public domain. Image from copy held at University of Toronto, available at archive.org.

Doodling frequently applies a similar associative formula to the visual realm. In Figure 31, for instance, Chesterton appears to doodle his way into a visual pun or portmanteau of Joseph Chamberlain and a pig. Likely beginning in the top right with his regular Chamberlain doodle – his third favourite doodle in 'The Notebook' after Gladstone and Thomas Huxley – it seems as if the nose arrests Chesterton's attention for he then repeats the doodle with several nasal variations. These in turn visually suggest something of a pig's snout, prompting a couple of pig doodles before the final composite image in the bottom centre of the page. Just as a rhyme compells his nonsense poem, visual affinity steers his doodling. Caught up in the simple pleasure of visual associations and kinaesthetic creation, the doodler experiences a kind of ecstasy that distances him from intentionality and individual consciousness and connects him to primal impulses. 'Between the hand and the trace', says Jean-Luc Nancy (2013), 'an impulse is tapped, an energy is gathered from an entire culture and history, an entire thought or experience of the world comes to be gathered in the vibration of the mark' (100–101). Just as language constrains speech so that we are in some sense 'possessed by it', the history of symbolic representation also constrains drawing. Instead of striving against this fact like so much art in the modern age, doodling gives into it, releasing the psychic tension connected with the need to be original and tapping into the stored up 'energy' of 'an entire culture and history'(Lecercle 25; Nancy 101).

Thus, both 'babble' and 'doodle' tell us something fundamental about the semiotic process. Nonsense is a useful analogue for doodling because it is a critically well-established genre that, like doodles, has at its structural core 'an unresolved tension between presence and absence of meaning', but is not therefore dismissed as 'indecipherable' by critics (Tigges 1988, 55). Perhaps not surprisingly, there is also a significant correlation between doodlers and nonsense writers. In addition to Lear and Chesterton, Thackeray's 'The Rose and the Ring' borders on the nonsensical along with other aspects of his comic writing, while Beerbohm's two favourite writers were Thackeray and Lear, and his writings – from his initial publication of *Works* to his humorous masterpiece *Zuleika Dobson* – sparkle with nonsensical moments.

The ludic impulse within doodling thus connects it with other light-hearted modes like the playful grotesque and the nonsensical while also gesturing to the

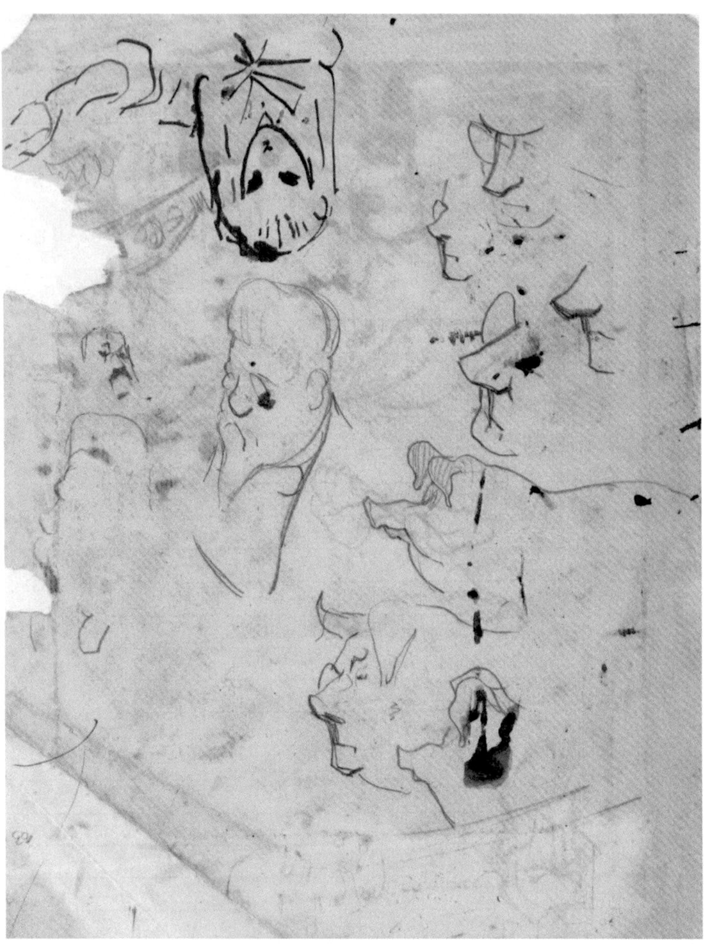

Figure 31 G. K. Chesterton, doodles of pigs, Joseph Chamberlain, and other figures (1894–6), BL Add MS 73334, page 83 recto (inverted). Image courtesy of the British Library. Reproduced by permission of United Agents Ltd on behalf of the Royal Literary Fund.

way in which doodling plays out post-structuralist insights about the fundamental irrationality of all signification. 'Reason', says Gilles Deleuze (2004), 'is always a region carved out of the irrational, not sheltered from the irrational at all, but traversed by it and only defined by a particular kind of relationship among irrational factors' (262). Our usual signs and symbols hide or obscure this fact giving us an illusion of semantic wholeness and autonomy, but 'underneath all reason lies delirium, and drift' (262). Doodling playfully unmasks our representational pretensions, revealing 'irrationality' as the bedrock of our 'rational' modes. In the process, doodling implicitly questions the very definitions of 'rational' and 'irrational', giving the bored or constrained mind a momentary carnival, a topsy-turvy realm where, to quote Emily Dickinson (1960), 'much sense' is 'the starkest madness' and 'much madness is divinest sense' (209).

Conclusion

This project began in earnest fifteen years ago. In our separate archival excavations, we had each stumbled upon troves of doodles by a surprising variety of nineteenth- and early twentieth-century authors. At the same time, we noticed that scholarship was largely silent about these odd, somewhat embarrassing marginalia. So we set out to do what academics are supposed to do: fill the lacuna with a quick scholarly article and get an easy publication. We soon discovered, however, that there is nothing quick or easy about studying doodles. As this Element has argued, doodles themselves are deceptively difficult to define, theorise, and interpret. In addition they are extremely challenging to find, access, and reproduce.

The question of whether a particular manuscript has doodles or whether an author doodled more generally is often hard to answer without costly, time-consuming archival research. Since critics have largely ignored or denigrated doodles, the typical scholarly apparatuses are rarely helpful, especially when their focus is on literature as opposed to visual art. Archival finding aids and catalogues rarely or inconsistently include 'doodle' in their metadata, preferring what are perceived as more neutral and respectable terms like 'sketches' or 'marginalia' or completely omitting to note the presence of doodles. 'Doodle' or 'doodling' are also unused in the indexes of biographies and scholarly works. Even when these books discuss how a writer doodled, as Peter Ackroyd (1995) does in *Blake*, 'doodle' does not appear in the index whereas entries like 'dilatoriness' and 'precognition' do (425).

Many critics seem to go out of their way to avoid the word 'doodle', often making even the full-text searching of digitised books fruitless. William Oddie (2008), for example, acknowledges how Chesterton 'drew, constantly, on any surface available' and cites how 'he absent-mindedly began to scribble a drawing of his fiancée on the wallpaper', but Oddie never describes this lifelong habit as 'doodling' or the products as 'doodles' (84). Instead, we have discovered many of the doodles in this Element (and our next Element) through accident, tangent, or rumour. For instance, someone serendipitously posted the Rossetti doodle of MacDonald one day on the George MacDonald Society Facebook page. This habit of sharing authors' doodles through social media, blog posts, and other information channels is common among scholars and librarians, suggesting that they are a source of interest and delight, just not of much scholarly interrogation.

Moreover, because authors' doodles typically reside in unpublished works and are rarely collated across authors, they are accessible only in widely disparate archival collections with a range of differing rules on handling the manuscripts and making or acquiring image reproductions. Likewise, the process of acquiring copyright permissions for unpublished manuscript material even for authors who have been dead for more than a hundred years is convoluted and expensive, and the fact that literary doodles occupy a liminal space between literary studies and art history means that there are few grants readily available for research visits or subventions.

Yet despite all these obstacles, we do not regret the time we have spent studying these transgressive entities. Their iconoclastic irreverence often baffles the critical endeavour, but in their resistance to easy interpretation, doodles consistently teach the value of patient, open, close attention. They break through the carefully wrought boundaries of typical scholarly discourse, and they have encouraged us to embrace more fallible, playful modes of reading and writing. Doodles are also delightful – they often shatter the solemnity of the academic enterprise and elicit uncensored laughter. We giggled far too frequently for archival decorum while turning Chesterton's notebooks sideways and upside down to get a better view of a pig.

Our hope is that by grappling with the definition of doodles, through comparisons with adjacent genres, and through exploring doodles' spectral, liminal, and ludic qualities, this Element will have somewhat lessened the structural difficulties of discussing doodles critically without diminishing the delightfulness of their creative chaos. Our forthcoming Element, *Literary Doodling in Britain, 1789–1930*, will further explore the elusive yet illuminating nature of doodles by tracing their evolution across various technological, cultural, and aesthetic contexts. Situating literary doodling within a broader historical framework, we will strive to illustrate how the doodling impulse has both reflected and resisted dominant trends in art, literature, and society. Together, we hope these Elements help to map some potential paths for others to enter the vibrant, untamed jungle of literary doodling.

References

Ackroyd, Peter. 1995. *Blake*. London: Sinclair-Stevenson.

Allen, Graham. 2021. 'Shelley as Visual Artist: Doodles, Sketches, Ink Blots, and the Critical Reception of the Visual'. *Studies in Romanticism* 60, no. 3 (Fall): 277–306.

Allingham, Philip V. 2012. '"Reading the Pictures, Visualizing the Text": Illustrations in Dickens from *Pickwick* to the *Household Edition*, 1836 to 1870, Phiz to Fred Barnard'. In *Reading Victorian Illustration, 1855–1875: Spoils of the Lumber Room*. Edited by Paul Goldman and Simon Cooke, 159–78. Farnham: Ashgate.

Andrade, Jackie. 2010. 'What Does Doodling Do?' *Applied Cognitive Psychology* 24, no. 1: 100–6.

Arundel, Russell M. 1937. *Everybody's Pixillated: A Book of Doodles*. Boston, MA: Little, Brown.

Bakhtin, Mikhail. 1984. *Rabelais and His World*. Bloomington: Indiana University Press.

Bambach, Carmen C. 1999. *Drawing and Painting in the Italian Renaissance Workshop: Theory and Practice, 1300–1600*. Cambridge: Cambridge University Press.

Barker, Dudley. 1973. *G. K. Chesterton: A Biography*. London: Constable.

Barsht, Konstantin. 2016. *The Drawings and Calligraphy of Fyodor Dostoevsky: From Image to Word*. Translated by Stephen Charles Frauzel. Bergamo: Lemma.

Barthes, Roland. 1977. *Image, Music, Text*. Translated by Stephen Heath. New York: Hill and Wang.

Battles, Matthew. 2004. 'In Praise of Doodling'. *The American Scholar* 73, no. 4: 105–8.

Beerbohm, Max. 1911. *Zuleika Dobson, or, An Oxford Love Story*. London: Heinemann.

1928. 'The Spirit of Caricature'. In *A Variety of Things*, 205–17. London: Heinemann.

1953. *Around Theatres*. London: Rupert Hart-Davis.

1964. *Letters to Reggie Turner*. Edited by Rupert Hart-Davis. London: Rupert Hart-Davis.

Briggs, Asa. 1998. 'Victorian Images of Gladstone'. In *Gladstone*. Edited by Peter J. Jagger, 33–49. London: Hambledon.

Brown, Sunni. 2014. *The Doodle Revolution: Unlock the Power to Think Differently*. New York: Portfolio/Penguin.

Bushell, Sally. 2009. *Text as Process: Creative Composition in Wordsworth, Tennyson, and Dickinson*. Charlottesville: University of Virginia Press.

Camille, Michael. 1992. *Image on the Edge: The Margins of Medieval Art*. Cambridge, MA: Harvard University Press.

Capra, Frank, director. 1936. *Mr. Deeds Goes to Town*. Columbia Pictures. 1 hr, 55 min. www.amazon.com/dp/B00RNV536K.

Capra, Fritjof. 2013. *Learning from Leonardo: Decoding the Notebooks of a Genius*. San Francisco, CA: Berrett-Koehler.

Carrier, David. 2000. *The Aesthetics of Comics*. University Park: Pennsylvania State University Press.

Chesterton, G. K. 1900. *Greybeards at Play*. London: R. Brimley Johnson.

(1935) 2012. 'The Victorian Debaters on Darwinism'. In *The Illustrated London News, 1935–1936*. Edited by Lawrence J. Clipper, 28–32. Vol. 37 of *The Collected Works of G. K. Chesterton*. Edited by George J. Marlin, Richard P. Rabatin, and John L. Swan. San Francisco, CA: Ignatius Press.

(1937) 1950. *Autobiography*. London: Hutchinson & Company.

Coleridge, Samuel Taylor. (1817) 2000. *Biographia Literaria*. In *Samuel Taylor Coleridge: The Major Works*. Edited by H. J. Jackson, 155–482. Oxford: Oxford University Press.

Culotta, Alexis. 2021. 'Preparatory Drawing During the Italian Renaissance, an Introduction'. *Smarthistory*. https://smarthistory.org/italian-renaissance-drawing.

Davis, Oliver. 'The Author at Work in Genetic Criticism'. *Paragraph* 25, no. 1 (March 2002): 92–106.

Davison, Sarah. 2011. 'Max Beerbohm's Altered Books'. *Textual Cultures* 6, no. 1 (Spring): 48–75.

Deleuze, Gilles. 2004. *Desert Islands and Other Texts, 1953–1974*. Translated by Michael Taormina. Los Angeles, CA: Semiotext(e).

Derrida, Jacques. 1976. *Of Grammatology*. Translated by Gayatri Chakravorty Spivak. Baltimore, MD: Johns Hopkins University Press.

1981. *Dissemination*. Translated by Barbara Johnson. Chicago, IL: University of Chicago Press.

1988. 'Signature Event Context'. In *Limited Inc*. Translated by Samuel Weber and Jeffrey Mehlman, 1–23. Evanston, IL: Northwestern University Press.

2001. *Writing and Difference*, 2nd ed. Translated by Alan Bass. London: Routledge.

2002. 'Spectrographies'. In *Echographies of Television*, by Jacques Derrida and Bernard Stiegler. Translated by Jennifer Bajorek, 113–34. Oxford: Polity.

Dickens, Charles. (1848) 1974. *Dombey and Son*. Edited by Alan Horsman. Oxford: Clarendon.

1977. *The British Academy/The Pilgrim Edition of the Letters of Charles Dickens, Vol. 4, 1844–1846*. Edited by Kathleen Mary Tillotson. Oxford: Clarendon.

Dickinson, Emily. 1960. *The Complete Poems of Emily Dickinson*. Edited by Thomas H. Johnson. Boston, MA: Little, Brown.

Dickson, Polly. 2022. 'Hoffmann's Signature Doodles'. *Literatur für Leser* 45, no. 1–2: 77–91.

Doherty, M. Stephen. 2005. 'Serious Doodles'. *American Artist* 69, no. 754 (May): 28–31.

Doran, Amanda-Jane. 2004. 'Landells, Ebenezer (1808–1860)'. *Oxford Dictionary of National Biography* online. https://doi.org/10.1093/ref:odnb/15971.

Felski, Rita. 2015. *The Limits of Critique*. Chicago, IL: University of Chicago Press.

Fennell, C. A. M., ed. 1892. *The Stanford Dictionary of Anglicised Words and Phrases*. Cambridge: Cambridge University Press.

Ferlazzo, Paul J. 2007. Review of *The Notebooks of Robert Frost*. *Choice* 44, no. 12 (August): 2106.

Freud, Ernst, Lucie Freud, and Ilse Grubrich-Simitis. 1978. *Sigmund Freud: His Life in Pictures and Words*. New York: Harcourt Brace Jovanovich.

Freud, Sigmund. 1960. *Jokes and Their Relation to the Unconscious*. Translated by James Strachey. New York: Norton.

Frow, John. 2015. *Genre*, 2nd ed. London: Routledge.

Frye, Northrup. 1990. *Anatomy of Criticism*. Princeton, NJ: Princeton University Press.

Gadamer, Hans-Georg. 2004. *Truth and Method*, 2nd ed. Translated by Joel Weinsheimer and Donald G. Marshall. London: Continuum.

Gennep, Arnold Van. 1960. *The Rites of Passage*. Translated by Monika B. Vizedom and Gabrielle L. Caffee. Chicago, IL: University of Chicago Press.

Gilchrist, Alexander. 1880. *Life of William Blake*, vol. I. London: MacMillan and Company.

Gilpin, William. 1792. *Three Essays: On Picturesque Beauty; On Picturesque Travel; And On Sketching Landscape*. London: Printed for R. Blamire.

Golden, Catherine. 2017. *Serials to Graphic Novels: The Evolution of the Victorian Illustrated Book*. Gainesville: University Press of Florida.

Goldman, Paul. 2012. 'Defining Illustration Studies: Towards a New Academic Discipline'. In *Reading Victorian Illustration, 1855–1875: Spoils of the Lumber Room*. Edited by Paul Goldman and Simon Cooke, 13–32. Farnham: Ashgate.

Goldman, Paul, and Simon Cooke, eds. 2012. *Reading Victorian Illustration, 1855–1875: Spoils of the Lumber Room*. Farnham: Ashgate.

Gombrich, E. H. 1991. Introduction: 'Caccia allo Scarabocchio'. In Zevola, *Piaceri di Noia*, 7–18.

1999. *The Uses of Images: Studies in the Social Function of Art and Visual Communication*. London: Phaidon.

Gombrich, E. H., and Ernst Kris. 1940. *Caricature*. Harmondsworth: Penguin.

Goslee, Nancy Moore. 1985. 'Shelley at Play: A Study of Sketch and Text in His "Prometheus" Notebooks'. *Huntington Library Quarterly* 48, no. 3 (Summer): 211–55.

2011. *Shelley's Visual Imagination*. Cambridge: Cambridge University Press.

Grego, Joseph. 1879. *Thackerayana: Notes and Anecdotes*. London: Chatto and Windus.

Gupta, Sharat. 2016. 'Doodling: The Artistry of the Roving Metaphysical Mind'. *Journal of Mental Health and Human Behaviour* 21, no. 1 (January–June): 16–19.

Hall, N. John. 1985. Introduction to *The Illustrated Zuleika Dobson, Or, An Oxford Love Story*, by Max Beerbohm. New Haven, CT: Yale University Press.

Hanks, Patrick. 2015. 'Definition'. In *The Oxford Handbook of Lexicography*. Edited by Philip Durkin, 94–122. Oxford: Oxford University Press.

Harvey, Robert C. 2009. 'How Comics Came to Be: Through the Juncture of Word and Image from Magazine Gag Cartoons to Newspaper Strips, Tools for Critical Appreciation plus Rare Seldom Witnessed Historical Facts'. In *A Comics Studies Reader*. Edited by Jeet Heer and Kent Worcester, 26–45. Jackson: University Press of Mississippi.

Haywood, Ian. 2013. *Romanticism and Caricature*. Cambridge: Cambridge University Press.

Henry Sotheran Ltd. 1879. *Sotheran's Price Current of Literature*, no. 177 (28 February): 4. https://hdl.handle.net/2027/mdp.39015076073827.

Hoffmann, E. T. A. 2004. 'The Artushof'. Translated by R. J. Hollingdale. In *Tales of Hoffmann*, selected by R. J. Hollingdale. London: Penguin.

Howard, Clifford. 1922. *Graphology*. Philadelphia: Pennsylvania Publishing Company.

Hughes, Daniel. 1970. 'Shelley, Leonardo, and the Monsters of Thought'. *Criticism* 12, no. 3 (Summer): 195–212.

Huizinga, Johan. (1944) 2007. *Homo Ludens: A Study of the Play-Element in Culture*. Abingdon: Routledge.

Hunt, Leigh. 1832. Preface to *The Masque of Anarchy: A Poem*, by Percy Bysshe Shelley, xiv–xv. London: Moxon.

Huxley, Aldous. 1955. 'Doodles in the Dictionary'. *Esquire* 44, no. 3 (September): 44–45, 135–36.

James, Philip. 1947. *English Book Illustration, 1800–1900*. London: Penguin.

Jenny, Laurent. 1996. 'Genetic Criticism and Its Myths'. Translated by Richard Watts. *Yale French Studies* 89 (Drafts): 9–25.

Jung, C. G. 1976. 'The Relations between the Ego and the Unconscious'. In *The Portable Jung*. Edited by Joseph Campbell, translated by R. F. C. Hull, 70–138. New York: Viking Press.

Junker, Howard. 1995. *The Writer's Notebook*. New York: HarperCollins.

King, Helen. 1957. *Your Doodles and What They Mean to You*. New York: Fleet.

Kooistra, Lorraine Janzen. 1995. *The Artist as Critic: Bitextuality in Fin-de-Siècle Illustrated Books*. Aldershot: Scholar Press.

Kristeva, Julia. 1982. *Powers of Horror: An Essay on Abjection*. New York: Columbia University Press.

Lauster, Martina. 2007. *Sketches of the Nineteenth Century: European Journalism and Its Physiologies, 1830–50*. Basingstoke: Palgrave.

Lawn, Chris, and Niall Keane. 2011. *The Gadamer Dictionary*. London: Continuum.

Lear, Edward. 1988. *Selected Letters*. Edited by Vivien Noakes. Oxford: Clarendon.

Lecercle, Jean-Jacques. 1994. *Philosophy of Nonsense: The Intuitions of Victorian Nonsense Literature*. London: Routledge.

Maclagan, David. 2014. *Line Let Loose: Scribbling, Doodling and Automatic Drawing*. London: Reaktion.

Marangoni, Kristen. 2013. 'Marginalized Modernisms: Doodling and Textual Production in the Works of Dylan Thomas, Samuel Beckett, and Stevie Smith'. PhD diss., University of Tulsa.

Marks, Claude. 1972. *From the Sketchbooks of the Great Artists*. New York: Crowell.

May, William. 2010. *Stevie Smith and Authorship*. Oxford: Oxford University Press.

Mercurio, Jeremiah Romano. 2011. 'Faithful Infidelity: Charles Ricketts's Illustrations for Two of Oscar Wilde's Poems in Prose'. *Victorian Network* 3, No. 1 (Special Bulletin): 3–21. https://doi.org/10.5283/vn.17.

Mercurio, Jeremiah Romano, and Daniel Gabelman. 2019. 'Literary Doodling in the Long Nineteenth Century: The Examples of

E. Cotton, G. K. Chesterton, and Max Beerbohm'. *Quærendo* 49, no. 1 (March): 3–35.

Mierlo, Wim Van. 2013. 'The Archaeology of the Manuscript: Towards Modern Palaeography'. In *The Boundaries of the Literary Archive: Reclamation and Representation*. Edited by Carrie Smith and Lisa Stead, 15–29. Farnham: Ashgate.

Morris, Charles. 1971. *Writings on the General Theory of Signs*. The Hague: Mouton.

Nancy, Jean-Luc. 2013. *The Pleasure in Drawing*. Translated by Philip Armstrong. New York: Fordham University Press.

Noakes, Vivien. 2004. *Edward Lear: The Life of a Wanderer*, rev. ed. London: Sutton.

Oddie, William. 2008. *Chesterton and the Romance of Orthodoxy: The Making of GKC, 1874–1908*. Oxford: Oxford University Press.

Pickering, Robert. 1997. 'Word, Pictorial Image and the Genesis of Writing in Paul Valéry's Cahiers'. *Word & Image* 13, no. 2 (April–June): 158–71.

Prescott-Steed, David. 2010. 'Doodle Culture: Meditations on the Great Idle Scrawl'. *Reconstruction: Studies in Contemporary Culture* 10, no. 2. http://reconstruction.digitalodu.com/Issues/102/recon_102_prescott-steed01.shtml.

Reid, Martine. 1994. 'Editor's Preface: Legible/Visible'. *Yale French Studies* 84 (Boundaries: Writing & Drawing): 1–12.

Ricketts, Charles. (1932) 2011. *Oscar Wilde: Recollections*. London: Pallas Athene.

Riquelme, Jean Paul. 2013. 'Oscar Wilde's Anadoodlegram: A Genetic, Performative Reading of *An Ideal Husband*'. In *Wilde Discoveries: Traditions, Histories, Archives*. Edited by Joseph Bristow, 289–314. Toronto: University of Toronto Press.

Rogers, Neville. 1967. *Shelley at Work: A Critical Inquiry*, 2nd ed. Oxford: Clarendon.

Ruskin, John. 1856–60. *Modern Painters*. 5 vols. London: Smith, Elder.

Sha, Richard C. 1998. *The Visual and Verbal Sketch in British Romanticism*. Philadelphia: University of Pennsylvania Press.

Smith, Stevie. 1974. 'Much Further Out Than You Thought', interview by Jonathan Williams. *Parnassus: Poetry in Review* 2, no. 2 (Spring/ Summer): 125–27.

Spacks, Patricia Meyer. 1995. *Boredom: The Literary History of a State of Mind*. Chicago, IL: University of Chicago Press.

Stillinger, Jack. 1994. *Coleridge and Textual Instability: The Multiple Versions of the Major Poems*. Oxford: Oxford University Press.

Sturgis, Matthew. 2018. *Oscar Wilde: A Life*. London: Head of Zeus.

Thompson, Henry L. 1899. *Henry George Liddell: D.D., Dean of Christ Church, Oxford. A Memoir*. London: John Murray.

Tigges, Wim. 1988. *An Anatomy of Literary Nonsense*. Amsterdam: Rodopi.

Todorov, Tzvetan. 1990. *Genres in Discourse*. Translated by Catherine Porter. Cambridge: Cambridge University Press.

Toohey, Peter. 2011. *Boredom: A Lively History*. New Haven, CT: Yale University Press.

Töpffer, Rodolphe. (1845) 1965. 'Essay on Physiognomy'. In *Enter the Comics*. Edited and translated by Ellen Wiese, 1–36. Lincoln: University of Nebraska Press.

Turner, Victor W. 1977. *The Ritual Process: Structure and Anti-structure*. Ithaca, NY: Cornell University Press. First published 1969 by Aldine Publishing (Chicago, IL).

1979. 'Betwixt and Between: The Liminal Period in *Rites de Passage*'. In *Reader in Comparative Religion*, 4th ed. Edited by W. A. Lessa, 234–43. New York: Harper & Row.

Viscusi, Robert. 1979. 'A Dandy's Diary: The Manuscripts of Max Beerbohm's *Zuleika Dobson*'. *The Princeton University Library Chronicle* 40, no. 3: 234–56.

Walker, Brian. 2022. 'Substance and Shadow: The Art of the Cartoon'. In *Comic Art in Museums*. Edited by K. A. Munson, 23–32. Jackson: University Press of Mississippi.

Ward, Maisie. 1944. *Gilbert Keith Chesterton*. London: Sheed & Ward.

Watts, Michael. 2000. *Doodle Interpretation: A Beginner's Guide*. Abingdon: Hodder & Stoughton.

Wilde, Oscar. 2000. *The Complete Works of Oscar Wilde, Vol. 1: Poems and Poems in Prose*. Edited by Bobby Fong and Karl Beckson. Oxford: Oxford University Press.

Wittgenstein, Ludwig. (1921) 2023. *Tractatus Logico-Philosophicus*. Translated by Michael Beaney. Oxford: Oxford University Press.

Wright, Thomas. 1875. *A History of Caricature and Grotesque in Literature and Art*. London: Chatto and Windus.

Zevola, Giuseppe. 1993. *Piaceri di Noia: Quattro Secoli di Scarabocchi nell'Archivio Storico del Banco di Napoli*. Milan: Leonardo.

Acknowledgements

We would like to thank the various libraries and archives that have made this research possible. Of special note are the following individuals and institutions whose generosity in providing image reproductions and publishing permissions has allowed us to represent the range of doodles and related drawings included in this book: Merlin Holland, Christopher MacDonald, Alastair 'Al' Murray, Charles Rossetti, the Estate of G.K. Chesterton, Dr Julia Walworth of Merton College Library and Archives (Oxford), Christ Church Library and Archives (Oxford), Princeton University Library, the Rare Book Department of the Free Library of Philadelphia, the Huntington Library, Houghton Library (Harvard), and the British Library.

Jeremiah would also like to thank and dedicate this monograph to his wife, Shawna, and son, Eli. Their enduring patience and support across many years of work on this and related projects has been invaluable and cherished.

Daniel would like to thank Marcus Waithe for his buzzing conversation and his cerebral honey, and dedicate this to the girl he was dating when he started studying doodles – for what still might be.

Cambridge Elements

Publishing and Book Culture

About the Series

This series aims to fill the demand for easily accessible, quality texts available for teaching and research in the diverse and dynamic fields of Publishing and Book Culture. Rigorously researched and peer-reviewed Elements will be published under themes, or 'Gatherings'. These Elements should be the first check point for researchers or students working on that area of publishing and book trade history and practice: we hope that, situated so logically at Cambridge University Press, where academic publishing in the UK began, it will develop to create an unrivalled space where these histories and practices can be investigated and preserved.

Printed in the United States
by Baker & Taylor Publisher Services